THE PURE LOVE OF MADAME GUYON

The Great Conflict in King Louis XIV's Court

Nancy C. James

University Press of America,® Inc.
Lanham · Boulder · New York · Toronto · Plymouth, UK

Copyright © 2007 by
Nancy C. James

University Press of America,® Inc.
4501 Forbes Boulevard
Suite 200
Lanham, Maryland 20706
UPA Acquisitions Department (301) 459-3366

Estover Road
Plymouth PL6 7PY
United Kingdom

All rights reserved
Printed in the United States of America
British Library Cataloging in Publication Information Available

Library of Congress Control Number: 2007925512
ISBN-13: 978-0-7618-3757-2 (paperback : alk. paper)
ISBN-10: 0-7618-3757-4 (paperback : alk. paper)

∞™ The paper used in this publication meets the minimum
requirements of American National Standard for Information
Sciences—Permanence of Paper for Printed Library Materials,
ANSI Z39.48—1984

For Roger and Hannah

Table of Contents

Preface	vii
Acknowledgements	ix
Introduction	xi
Chapter One. Historical Perspective on the Great Conflict	1
Chapter Two. Madame Guyon's Interior Life	25
Chapter Three. Guyon's Theology of the Holy Spirit	39
Chapter Four. A University of Oxford Manuscript about Madame Guyon	57
Chapter Five. Madame Guyon: Spirituality for Extreme Times	69
Afterword by the Rev. John M. Graham	81
Appendix. The Oxford Manuscript Translated: *Supplement to the Life of Madame Guyon*	85
Notes	105
Bibliography	115
Index	117
About the Author	121

Preface

In my study of religious mysticism, I found myself returning to the rich theology of Madame Guyon again and again. Her words were born in the crucible of suffering from her nearly decade long incarceration and in her active life of service to the poor. In her struggle for human rights, she founded hospitals, successfully argued legal cases, and cared for her large family. Madame Guyon's natural authority and spirituality attracted many in seventeenth and eighteenth century France and then in the wider world. Her ideas still challenge us with her belief in pure love and spiritual annihilation. The deathless fire of pure love, she writes, calls us to lofty goals that lead us to fulfillment.

This book was born out of my questions taken to Guyon's theology and somehow sensing traces of the sublime in her writing.

The afterword is written by the Rev. John M. Graham. His understanding of the mystical element in modern philosophy provides a strong intellectual framework in which to place Madame Guyon's theology.

I thank my students for engaging in discussion about these ideas of Madame Guyon and Archbishop Fénelon. I also appreciate all the dialogue in conferences, retreats, and religious institutions where I have been honored to present the theology of Madame Jeanne Guyon.

Nancy C. James
Day of Saint Michael and All Angels
September 29, 2006
Washington, D.C.

Acknowledgements

I want to thank Elly Sparks Brown and Hugh Brown for their conversations about pure love. I also appreciate Augusta Ogden and her discussions about book development.

I thank Roger and Hannah for all their help during the writing of this book.

I want to thank the parishioners of St. John's Episcopal Church, Lafayette Square, and Grace Church, Georgetown, for their dialogue about our rich spiritual tradition.

The picture of Madame Guyon on the cover is by an unknown artist. The drawing originally appeared in *Little Journeys to the Homes of the Great* by Elbert Hubbard published by The Roycrofters in 1916.

Acknowledgements

I want to thank Elly Sparks Brown and Hugh Brown for their conversations about pure love. I also appreciate Augusta Ogden and her discussions about book development.

I thank Roger and Hannah for all their help during the writing of this book.

I want to thank the parishioners of St. John's Episcopal Church, Lafayette Square, and Grace Church, Georgetown, for their dialogue about our rich spiritual tradition.

The picture of Madame Guyon on the cover is by an unknown artist. The drawing originally appeared in *Little Journeys to the Homes of the Great* by Elbert Hubbard published by The Roycrofters in 1916.

Introduction

During the powerful reign of King Louis XIV, a controversy called the Great Conflict raged about the validity of mystical experiences. Madame Guyon, an aristocratic French woman, wrote theological treatises about the interior life lived with God. This mystical theology brought her to the attention of King Louis XIV, his secret wife Madame de Maintenon, and the most powerful clerics in France. An explosive controversy ensued over whether Madame Guyon truly experienced the divine presence. One prominent cleric, Bishop Bossuet, publicly attacked Guyon's advocate, Archbishop Fénelon, about Madame Guyon's veracity. The steadfast Archbishop defended Guyon, even as his career was destroyed by Bishop Bossuet. This political struggle led to trouble in King Louis' court at Versailles, political intrigue in the Vatican, and the unfortunate incarceration of Madame Guyon in the Bastille.

The controversy over Madame Guyon continued after her death. Privately in the intimacy of King Louis' court at Versailles, Duc de Saint-Simon secretly recorded his first-hand witness of the inner workings of Louis and his advisors in his three-volume work, *Historical Memoirs*. Because of their shocking content, these memoirs were hidden, until Voltaire championed the cause of their publication in the eighteenth century. Duc de Saint-Simon wrote extensively about the controversy over Madame Guyon.

Duc de Saint-Simon exposed much about Louis' court at Versailles, including the influences behind his decisions. The duke revealed the controversy that swirled around Louis' secret marriage to the governess for his children, who came to be known as Madame de Maintenon. Saint-Simon attributes some of Louis' worst decisions to Maintenon's influence, including the Revocation of the Edict of Nantes leading to the death of many French Protestants and the lengthy War of The Spanish Succession. According to Duc de Saint-Simon, Madame de Maintenon also motivated the lengthy controversy over Madame Guyon and the form of mysticism called Quietism.

In the eighteenth century after Madame Guyon's death, an anonymous French author wrote an interpretation of her life and ministry. He probably did not identify his name because of fear of incarceration or death. This author attacked the accepted version of Madame de Maintenon's life written by La Beaumelle, a novelist who wrote a imaginative version of King Louis' court.

This anonymous author's insightful document adds historical information about this important era in history, as well as a probing interpretation of Guyon's life and those surrounding her. In particular, the author analyzes the powerful Bishop Bousset's ferocious attack on Madame Guyon and Archbishop Fénelon's intense defense of her.

Voltaire himself had written a history of Louis XIV's era. Voltaire adamantly criticized La Beaumelle's forgeries of Madame de Maintenon's letters and was the primary advocate of publishing Duc de Saint-Simon's historical memoirs. The anonymous author adds new information and interpretation about this struggle while offering theological insights about this conflict.

In *The Pure Love of Madame Guyon: The Great Conflict in King Louis XIV's Court* this historical document is translated for the first time from the original, handwritten French. This crucial document exposes the Great Conflict and the powerful influence this controversy over mysticism has had on history and theology. Madame Guyon's work is analyzed and her valuable contributions are acknowledged. Madame Guyon wrote a theology of the Holy Spirit from a unique perspective. Madame Guyon's mystical theology, with its acceptance of diversity and ecumenism, now also speaks to our own issues in the twenty-first century.

Chapter One

Historical Perspective on the Great Conflict

In France in the late 1600s a major church controversy developed about the validity of mystical experience that eventually demanded the attention of Pope Innocent XII. This controversy known as "The Great Conflict" swirled around three important and influential persons, the Archbishop of Cambrai, François de Salignac de la Mothe Fénelon, a noble laywoman Madame Jeanne Bouvier de la Motte Guyon, and the Bishop of Meaux, Jacques Benigne Bossuet. The direct intervention of King Louis XIV and his secret wife, Madame de Maintenon, caused this impassioned dispute to escalate precipitously, drawing the attention of many throughout Europe. Ecclesiastics wrote volumes about all aspects of this controversy, while many European aristocrats vigorously debated the moral, religious, and spiritual issues involved with it. A committee of cardinals was eventually commissioned by Pope Innocent XII to consider all aspects of this dramatic disagreement over this particular type of mysticism, which came to be known as "Quietism."

The painful effects of this controversy were many. Bishop Bossuet, who had been Fénelon's mentor and who consecrated him as an archbishop, developed into a bitter enemy of his former pupil. Madame Guyon, who had once been a wealthy, influential widow found herself incarcerated in various prisons, including the infamous Bastille. Archbishop Fénelon, who had been expected to become a cardinal, was forcibly kept within the confines of his Diocese of Cambrai and forbidden to travel outside his diocese by Louis XIV. Guyon's spiritual director, Father La Combe, who had expected to become a famous preacher, became insane after his life-long imprisonment. Madame de Maintenon struggled with her husband Louis XIV as she first welcomed Madame Guyon and then asked him for Madame Guyon's incarceration. Relationships were strained and damaged among many of the most dominant and powerful persons in the French court. Bishop Bossuet charged both Guyon and Fénelon with heresy and attempted to destroy them through a lengthy campaign requesting their condemnations from Pope Innocent XII. Louis XIV, also known as the Sun King, personally watched and participated in this long crisis. He demanded the condemnation of one of Fénelon's books, widening a chasm between the French Roman Catholic Church and the papacy.

What could be seen as a conflict that should have remained within the court of Louis XIV became part of an even larger theological argument that was raging in Europe, the controversy over Quietism. The issue underlying this long, painful controversy was whether the form of mysticism called Quietism, and the spirituality expounded in that thought, should be condemned as a heresy or accepted as a valid path to the direct experience of God.

What came to be called Quietism was an approach to prayer that held that spiritual perfection can be achieved in this world by accepting a union with God. This perfection comes through a passive listening for God's word in the soul, a word which purifies and enlightens as it is delivered. The person expresses faith about God's willingness to act by listening intently for the divine spirit, and at the reception of the word, acting upon any divine inspirations that accompany the word. In these respects, Quietism had much in common with mainstream Catholic spirituality.1

For Quietists, the crucial factor in finding a union with God is the annihilation or transformation of the individual will. God's will presents both the ultimate joy and the highest human calling. The Holy Spirit annihilates the person's individual will so that the person participates in this divine will. The will of God grants blessings to the believer. As the famous Quietist Molinos wrote: "Be constant, O happy Soul, be constant and of good courage; for however intolerable thou art to thy self, yet thou wilt be protected, enriched and beloved by that greatest Good, as if He had nothing else to do, than to lead thee to perfection, by the highest ways of love."2

In Quietist thought all situations in the world may be used for the good of the eternal soul. Both sufferings and joys may bring the person closer to God, and an intimate sense of God's presence may be enjoyed no matter what the life circumstances are. Madame Guyon wrote in a letter about this,

> Rest assured, it is the same God who causes the scarcity and the abundance, the rain and the fair weather. The high and low states, the peaceful and the state of warfare, are each good in their season. These vicissitudes form and mature the interior, as the different seasons compose the year. . . . God loves you; let this thought equalise all states. Let him do with us as with the waves of the sea, and whether he takes us to his bosom, or casts us upon the sand, that is, leave us to our own barrenness, all is well.3

In Quietism God's ultimate being is gracious. Because of this divine character, the person, dwelling in utter trust, experiences an indifference about situations, as well as an indifference to the state of personal salvation. This indifference is based on the belief that God's will is good and merciful, hence God's will is to be desired above all else. No one is to fear or shun the realization of God's will, even to the ultimate question of whether the soul will enjoy God's presence for eternity or be banished from this presence. So for most Quietist thinkers, the quality of indifference over situations should extend to the person's salvation. The believer trusts God deeply and leaves the state of his or her eternal salvation to the responsibility of God. This type of indifference is founded on the belief that God's ultimate judgment about the state of the soul is good and trustworthy. The believer is freed from all anxiety and care about the salvation of his or her soul.

This seeming indifference to individual salvation that is attained through obedience to the church outraged some, including Bishop Bossuet, and was a deciding factor in the condemnation of Quietism by the Roman Catholic Church. Madame Guyon describes the mental process she experienced in her own indifference to her salvation. "It appeared to me then, O my God, that I was offered the choice either of the approbation of men and success, together with the assurance of my salvation; or of the cross, wretchedness, rejection, persecution from all creatures, even privation of all creatures, even privation of all assurance of salvation, and nothing but your glory alone. O love, the latter was the object of my choice and of my tender inclination."[4]

Quietism as a way of life is found in all major religions. Viktor Conzemius writes that this loosely-knit body of thought is "found in all the higher religions" and cites examples of Quietism as including Lao-Tse in the Tao, Zen Buddhism, Stoicism, and Neo-Platonism.[5] Quietism in these religions and philosophies is a passive attitude towards life that emphasizes contemplation and a total emptying of the individual will. An example of Quietist thinking is found in the fourteenth century writings of Marguerite Porete in what is called the Free Spirit heresy. She was burned at the stake in 1310 for advocating her thought about annihilation of the soul. Porete wrote about these spiritual persons, saying that they were,

> Annihilated in all things through Humility.
> At peace in divine being through divine will.
> She who wills nothing except divine will.[6]

The main proponent of Quietism in the Roman Catholic Church was the Spanish priest Miguel de Molinos (1640-1697), author of *The Spiritual Guide Which Disentangles the Soul*, first published in 1675. Molinos lived in Rome from 1664, working as a popular spiritual director and priest who guided many into a contemplative life. He advocated a passivity to God and to God's will that has been called indifference. Acting upon his advice, some nuns under his spiritual direction gave up saying the rosary and stopped observing certain devotions in the convents, which caused Molinos to come under suspicion. He was suddenly arrested on July 18, 1685, and charged with heresy. Molinos' former friend, Pope Innocent XI, condemned his beliefs as heretical in a papal bull on November 19, 1687, titled "Coelestis Pastor." In the bull Pope Innocent XI takes sixty-eight propositions of Molinos' and declares them heretical. Molinos was condemned to life imprisonment.

The following is the beginning of the Bull of Innocent XI against Molinos in which are listed the condemned beliefs.

> 1. That it is necessary that a man annihilate his own powers and talent and this is the internal road. Condemned.
> 2. To want to work actively is to offend God. Condemned.

3. The desires about something needing to be done are impediments of perfection. Condemned.7

What were the problems with Quietism? Many of those associated with Quietism withdrew from sacramental and devotional practices, as happened to those whom Molinos counseled. This disrupted the sacramental order of the church and called into question the necessity and power of the church sacraments. George P. Fisher says, "The real ground of hostility to Quietism was its tendency to lead to the dispensing with auricular confession and penances and outward rites altogether."8

A second concern about Quietism is the ethical positions that result from following this passive attitude. The popular perception in the Roman Catholic Church was that the Quietists thought that whatever they did was acceptable because behavior didn't matter. Many Quietists were charged with sexual immorality, including Molinos and Guyon, although the historical accuracy of these charges is highly questionable. Invalid charges of sexual immorality had also been made against "Free Spirits" in the fourteenth century.9

The situation of the French church in which this divisive crisis occurred was a turbulent one. In the sixteenth century the Protestant Reformation had swept through Europe and many countries had split off from the Roman Catholic Church. Some feared that France would leave the Roman Catholic Church after they formed the Gallican movement in the 1600s that denied the pope ultimate spiritual authority in France.

Within the French Roman Catholic Church, divisions between powerful groups caused turbulent struggles for power and influence. The Jansenist movement in the church had led to controversy among church and state leaders. Cornelius Jansen, bishop of Ypres, wrote a treatise called *Augustinus*, in which divine grace is understood as an irresistible force which formed the human being by a supernatural determinism. People needed a special grace from God to perform His commandments for the human will was not sufficiently strong to seek God naturally. The human soul was predestined for eternal salvation or damnation by God.10

Jansenists placed a high value on confession in contradistinction to the Quietists shunning of sacramental rites. They emphasized personal piety and felt that the individual should actively seek salvation and moral reform through intellectual striving and intense introspection. Their high standards for human existence separated them from the remainder of the church as they called for stringent behavior in what they saw as a church and society filled with lax morality. Because of these beliefs, they deeply involved themselves with state politics and attempted to place their candidates in court positions. They strongly supported the rights of French bishops in opposition to the papacy, the movement known as Gallicanism. In brief, Jansenism was a movement filled with self-confidence; and its members had the assurance of knowing what the future direction of the church should be.

Jansenists opposed Quietism, and hence struggled against Guyon and Fénelon. Guyon believed that grace could be resisted, saying that in her own life, she had rejected God's grace many times. The Jansenist's belief in the active striving of the individual for salvation was also diametrically opposed to the Quietist indifference to salvation. But the Jansenists, too, found themselves in trouble. The Roman Catholic Church declared Jansenism a heresy in 1653 when five propositions of Cornelius Jansen were condemned by Pope Innocent X in the Bull "Cum Occasione." Alexander Sedgwick writes about this condemnation, "The Catholic Church found the elitism inherent in Jansenist belief objectionable because salvation appeared to be inaccessible to the ordinary mortal."[11]

Another group that became involved in this tempestuous situation were the Jesuits, an order that had great power in France because they supplied the king's confessor. The Jansenists believed, as did others, that the Jesuit's moral and ethical standards were less strict than they should be. The Jesuits applied moral principles to determine right or wrong in particular situations, a discipline known as casuistry. Their sophisticated understanding of moral subtleties frequently caused them to view moral choices as very complex, and to assign culpability for sin on a sliding scale according to circumstances. Their acceptance of the difficulty of making complex moral judgments with precision was seen by some as a dangerous compromise that led to a lowering of ethical standards. The Jesuits, in fact, sought popularity in France through relaxing moral standards, in hopes of making the Roman Catholic Church more acceptable to persons who saw Christianity as having impossibly high moral standards. The Jansenists attacked the Jesuits and their casuistry, believing that they destroyed the essential moral character of Christianity by lowering its ethical principles.

Many criticized Father de la Chaise, King Louis XIV's Jesuit confessor, for his acceptance of Louis XIV's behavior. King Louis received the Eucharist at appointed times during the year. Members of his court wondered how could this be happening when he has public mistresses. Who was giving Louis absolution in his confession? Some historians think that the Jesuits made special rules for Louis that told him that his duty was to produce heirs through his wife. As long as he produced heirs, then he was allowed extra-marital, monogamous affairs with other women. Many thought that Louis' behavior should have excluded him from the Eucharist and the fact that it did not, opened the church to ridicule. Archbishop Fénelon wrote that Father de la Chaise was "afraid of sound virtue and likes only profane and loose people."[12]

The Jesuits' active pursuit of salvation through the meditation techniques written about in the *Spiritual Exercises* of St. Ignatius of Loyola differed from the indifferent Quietist approach to this issue. Guyon opposed this active method of seeking God, and found herself at times in opposition to the Jesuits during these years of controversy. Guyon, though, idealistically hoped that her plight would move the Jesuit confessor of King Louis XIV, Father de la Chaise, to help her, even though they had differing theological beliefs. In her *Autobiography* Guyon tells of sending a letter to Father de la Chaise, asking him for help only to be denied assistance from him. The theological divisions in France remained in place and could not be bridged, even by an incarcerated Guyon who begged for assistance.

In the seventeenth century, the French Roman Catholic Church was still struggling to mend and overcome the damage done by the sixteenth century Protestant Reformation, while at the same time it was forced to respond to internal controversy. The major participants in this situation had all played a part in responding to the Protestant challenge to the safety of the Roman Catholic Church.

Fénelon spent much of his early career converting Protestants to Catholicism, advocating gentle treatment as a means of inducing them to return to the Catholic Church. This was a radical policy considering the violent history of France towards its Protestants. The sixteenth century lengthy Wars of Religion against the Huguenots culminated in the 1572 massacre on St. Bartholomew's Day with the murder of about 8,000 Protestants in Paris. Tens of thousands of Protestants were killed throughout France in the following weeks. In 1598 Henry the IV issued the Edict of Nantes that assured Protestants safety when they lived in certain areas. On October 18, 1685, Louis XIV revoked the Edict of Nantes. This revocation allowed violence to once again threaten the Protestant's safety and destroy any cooperation that existed between the two groups. Bishop Bossuet fully supported this revocation of the Edict of Nantes.

The Roman Catholic Church retained the full structure and power of the Inquisition during this period of history. If a person was found guilty of heresy, incarceration for life or death by burning at the stake could result. The severity of these punishments instilled a dread of being labeled a Quietist because this could bring about the destruction of life and freedom. In Guyon's *Autobiography* she writes of her inquisitors' threats of "death, the scaffold," and "perpetual imprisonment" on numerous occasions.13

Dramatis Personae

The central person in this controversy was Jeanne Marie Bouvier de La Motte Guyon who lived from 1648 until 1717. Madame Guyon documents her entire life in her *Autobiography*. Jeanne lived a difficult life as a child and teenager. Her mother was a cold and distant woman who largely ignored her and deprived her of many normal childhood activities such as regular educational and social opportunities. Although her mother "did not much love girls," Jeanne de La Motte compensated for this by spending much of her time reading the Bible and religious books.14 Jeanne's mother claimed to have religious responsibilities at the church that interfered with the care of her daughter. This neglect obviously made an impression on Jeanne de La Motte, who wrote later in life about this, saying that using church responsibilities as an excuse not to care for children causes serious damage to children and should not be done.

Jeanne's father was a widower with children when he married her mother. The family never successfully developed into a unified group. Jeanne felt concerned about her relationships with her older siblings because of the tensions in the family. Conflicts frequently erupted both in her parent's marriage and the relationships among the siblings. Indeed, Jeanne's elder half-brother, a member of the Barnabite order, later initiated one of the first persecutions against her.

Jeanne de La Motte, nonetheless, became a charming and attractive teenager who drew the attentions of her family and friends, causing her life to change into a more pleasant one. As a result of this, her mother started to involve herself more with Jeanne's life and interested herself in her daughter's social events. Jeanne de La Motte developed normally, becoming interested in romantic love and avidly reading romance novels, a habit which she forced herself to break later in life. As a youth Jeanne also reports thoroughly reading the spiritual works of St. Francis de Sales, St. Jane de Chantal, and Lorenzo Scupoli's *Spiritual Warfare*. Jeanne's father allowed her the freedom of spontaneous conversation at social events and her reputations spread as an intelligent conversationalist. Through the years of Jeanne's lonely childhood, she developed an active imagination and a quick mind. These charming qualities drew persons to her, even as Jeanne enjoyed her quiet reverence for God. Throughout her life Jeanne de La Motte sought plentiful hours of rich solitude.

Then tragedy struck Jeanne de La Motte. Jeanne's father arranged what was an extremely unhappy marriage from the start. At age fifteen she was forced into marrying a wealthy widower with high social standing, who at the time of the marriage, February 18, 1664, was thirty-eight years old. Monsieur Guyon was the son of the constructor of the Canal of Briare that connected the basins of the River Loire and River Seine.

Jeanne's horror at the marriage is made clear in her *Autobiography* where she wrote that she "wept bitterly" during the wedding ceremony and celebrations, for Jeanne desired to become a nun.(43) She yearned to dedicate herself to divine love, which was denied by the reality of this ill-conceived marriage.

Soon after her wedding, the young Madame Guyon's life became filled with abuse. Her husband Jacques disliked Jeanne's temperament. Though he physically desired Guyon, her personality was not pleasing to him. Monsieur Guyon wanted a submissive and quiet wife but her personality heretofore had been outgoing and charming. He hoped for Guyon to partake in religion only with moderation but she was quite fervent in her beliefs. He desired for her to be interested only in him while Guyon's lively mind led her to an active intellectual interests.

A struggle began at home with Guyon's mother-in-law and her husband actively trying to change Guyon. They developed strict rules which Guyon followed involving restricted church attendance, limited prayer, and little time for reading. Her social conversations were monitored and forced to be brief. As if this was not stifling enough, Guyon received constant and severe criticisms about her behavior. Guyon responded by becoming detached from the world around her and praying constantly. In her own words, she developed an "alienation from the corruption of the century."(63)

This inward withdrawal led to serious problems for Guyon. She developed many illnesses and became terrified of speaking. Because of this, the strict rules were tightened even further. During this tense and unhappy marriage, Guyon bore five children, two of whom died as young children. She states in her *Autobiography* that her husband and mother-in-law alienated some of her children from her. The tension in the home continued to escalate, and Guyon describes this in her *Autobiography*, "O my God, how wearisome without you would be a life like that!" (138)

At the age of nineteen Madame Guyon talked to a monk about her despair and he counseled looking inwardly for the presence of God. She developed an intense personal devotion to God. Her spiritual journey is described in more detail in subsequent chapters.

An unexpected blow later threw the Guyon family into a crisis. Monsieur Guyon developed serious financial problems after Louis XIV's brother tried to obtain the Guyon fortune under false pretences. Madame Guyon's own brother helped this member of the French royalty in this plot to illegally gain the Guyon money. Monsieur Guyon told his intelligent wife about the detailed legal case. Madame Guyon assured him that she could win this case and surprisingly Monsieur Guyon accepted her offer of assistance. Madame Guyon successfully argued a legal case to the judges involved with the case and thus saved the Guyon fortune. This victory helped create a rapprochement between the conflicted couple with Monsieur Guyon looking at his wife with new appreciation.(163)

Monsieur Guyon's health eventually collapsed as he suffered from gout and other illnesses. Madame Guyon nursed her husband with care and her husband appreciated her ministry. Before he died on July 21, 1676, he offered an apology to Guyon by saying "I did not deserve you."15

Guyon was left as an attractive, wealthy widow. Following the death of her husband, Guyon stayed initially with her mother-in-law but the estrangement in their family relationships ended this situation. Guyon's two sons went to live with other relatives. Guyon kept her young daughter with her and traveled to live quietly in rented houses and to stay with friends. Guyon spent time in Paris and contemplated her uncertain future. Her obligations to her family and estate were complicated by the lack of relief from the support of a family structure.

What was Guyon to do? Her relationships with many of her relatives were strained because of the abuse she had endured. Fortunately Guyon found a capable spiritual director with the priest, Father François La Combe. His main characteristics of "simplicity and straightforwardness" made him a trustworthy person for Guyon. (290)

Having found satisfaction in nursing her husband, the next natural step for Guyon was to develop a life healing the sick. When Father La Combe moved to a ministry in the area of Geneva, Guyon developed an overwhelming sense of God calling her to minister to others in the same area. She invented medicinal ointments and used them for those who had no access to physicians. To accomplish this ministry, Guyon moved with her five-year-old daughter to the area surrounding Geneva.

Almost immediately upon her arrival, Guyon once again found herself embroiled in controversy. Guyon had placed her money in trust for her children; however, the bishop of Geneva, Jean D'Aranthon, wished for her to donate substantial amounts of her money to the church. Guyon refused to comply. In an attempt to gain control over her, the bishop devised a plan for her to become a mother superior of a religious order called the *Nouvelles Catholiques*.16 Guyon adamantly refused this idea also, saying that her lack of religious vows made the offer ludicrous. Rumors developed about Guyon and La Combe's relationship;

Guyon wrote that "they circulated a story that I was running about with him . . . and a hundred malicious absurdities."17

Guyon's problems were further exacerbated when she protected a young nun against the sexual advances of a corrupt church official, whom Guyon only identifies as the "Little Bishop" because he was a close friend of Bishop D'Aranthon. Guyon writes that the nun "recognized that to connect herself with that ecclesiastic was something imperfect." Guyon further writes that the ecclesiastic "was the source of all the persecutions that befell me."18

Even during these times, though, Madame Guyon cared for the sick and established several hospitals for the poor. Her ministry thrived among both the peasants and the wealthy.

This intercession for the young nun, the gossip about her relationship with La Combe and her widespread popularity among some clergy eventually led to Guyon and La Combe's expulsion from this diocese. La Combe and Guyon left, starting a meandering five year journey through different parts of Europe, traveling both separately and together, making few plans about which cities to visit and what to do when they arrived at their destinations. Guyon believed that divine providence directed her ways and that God would care for her needs. Guyon said she spent "every day in uncertainty."(30) She interpreted her situation as a necessary mortification that accompanies an intimate relationship with God. She writes about this in her *Autobiography*.

> But for those who give themselves up to God without any reserve, and who are willing with all their hearts to be the plaything of providence without restriction or reserve——ah, as for those, they are assuredly a spectacle for God, for angels, and for men: for God, of glory, by the conformity with Jesus Christ; for angels, of joy; and for men, of cruelty and disgrace.(64)

Guyon and La Combe traveled widely in their new ministry. Upon arrival in a new city, usually at the invitation of a bishop, La Combe frequently would be hired for a prestigious position, while Guyon stayed with aristocratic women. Many sought Guyon's spiritual counsel.

Troubles developed as her reputation for spiritual wisdom spread. Church officials grew alarmed and said that a female spiritual leader upsets the church structure. Guyon wrote that some monks were "vexed that a woman . . . should be so sought after."(85) Some called her a witch and said that Guyon was a "sorceress" and "diabolic."(98) Consequently she was asked to leave place after place. Out of necessity, Father La Combe and Madame Guyon moved frequently. Among the places they visited were Thonon, Turin, Grenoble, Marseilles, Nice, Genoa, and Vercelli. Rumors circulated that Guyon and La Combe might be having a physical relationship. Both La Combe and Guyon steadfastly denied these charges, saying that they were in the role of confessor-penitent with each other.

The traveling of Father La Combe accompanied by Madame Guyon fulfilled the priest's theology that he called "laissez faire Dieu." He believed that God acts when a person receives in quiet contemplation the inspirations of God.

Laissez faire God means to let God have the freedom to do with the individual what God wills. God plans and takes the person to whatever ministry is needed. La Combe writes,

> If we aspire after Christian perfection, we must disengage ourselves, and forego all that concerns our own interest, to have God alone in view. This is the generous charity; this is the purity of love. All self-interested motives are imperfect, because in them we seek ourselves. Walk in the most excellent way, which is that of disinterestedness.19

Father de La Mothe, Guyon's half-brother and La Combe's superior in the Barnabite order, caused additional problems for them by the accusations of moral improprieties. Father de La Mothe wrote many church officials complaining about La Combe's alleged scandalous behavior with Guyon. Father La Mothe also accused La Combe of Quietism, showing church officials "propositions . . . of Molinos, saying they were the errors of Father La Combe."(143) Despite the absence of a legal right to benefit from the Guyon money, Father La Mothe criticized Guyon's handling of her own finances.

After five years of La Combe and Guyon's journeys, Father La Mothe devised a malicious plan. He extended an invitation to Father La Combe to preach in Paris, while secretly arranging La Combe's personal Inquisition. Rumors were spread that La Combe was having secret dealings with Rome which was a serious charge from the Gallican hierarchy. Guyon recognized that her half-brother meant harm to La Combe, but La Combe insisted on returning in order to fulfill his vows of obedience. He was arrested on October 3, 1687, and began his life-long incarceration. Father La Mothe was able to "persuade His Majesty that he is a dangerous spirit; therefore, without judging him, he has been shut up in a fortress for his life."(159) La Combe was imprisoned for heresy for twenty-seven years. His incarceration ended only with his death in 1715.

La Combe lost everything following his arrest. He was forced to leave behind his ministry and his world of ideas. He was moved frequently in his incarceration in order that he not receive any favoritism from jailors. His places of incarceration include a prison farm, the castle at Vincennes, and the dreaded Bastille.

Madame Guyon had repeatedly tried to help Father La Combe by giving him advice and spiritual nourishment. Father La Combe rejected much of Guyon's advice on the political situation in the church because he believed that his ecclesiastical superiors were earnestly seeking the truth and would grow to understand that he was orthodox in his beliefs. Madame Guyon continued to support Father La Combe during his incarceration and states in her *Autobiography* that she believed that Father La Combe would have a special reward in heaven because of his intense suffering for righteousness sake. Guyon wrote about Father La Combe, saying, "God, who sees all, will render to each according to his works. I know by the spirit communication that he is very content and abandoned to God."(159)

Now Guyon could expect the same unfortunate fate as Father La Combe. On January 29, 1688, Guyon received a *lettre de cachet*, a letter from the French king ordering her imprisonment. Louis XIV commanded that she be incarcerated at the Visitation Convent in the Rue Saint-Antoine in Paris. The royal letter stated that Guyon had correspondence with Miguel de Molinos who was a condemned heretic, and, because of this association, she was also a suspect.

Guyon was held in a small room without windows and held under constant supervision. Guyon submitted to the incarceration during which she was questioned about her beliefs by the Archbishop's chancellor and others. Guyon was offered her freedom if she consented to the marriage of her heiress daughter to the nephew of Archbishop Harlay. Madame Guyon immediately refused this offer, preferring to stay incarcerated than to arrange a marriage for her child. (206) For the next eight months, outside groups worked both for her release and for her continued confinement. Finally, because of the intervention of Madame de Maintenon with her husband Louis XIV, an order for Guyon's release came on August 24, 1688.

About six weeks after her release, Madame Guyon met Father Fénelon at a social gathering. He had heard much about Guyon and showed an interest in her theology. They quickly became spiritually close, partaking in lengthy conversations and frequent correspondences. She wrote about this, "Some days after my release, having heard mention of the Abbé de Fénelon . . . I was suddenly with extreme force and sweetness interested for him. It seemed to me our Lord united him to me very intimately, more so than any one else. The next day I had the opportunity of seeing him. . . . It seems to me that my soul has perfect rapport with him."(218-219)

Others also experienced rapport with Madame Guyon. Madame de Maintenon invited Madame Guyon to teach her method of prayer at her school at Saint Cyr for the daughters of the war-ruined, impoverished nobility. Guyon's theology from *A Short and Easy Method of Prayer* spread throughout the school and influenced the adolescent students. Eventually though this caused even more trouble for Madame Guyon.

Some clerics who came to Saint-Cyr became concerned about Guyon and her methods, calling them Quietist. The bishop of Chartres and Saint-Cyr, Paul Godet, told Madame de Maintenon that Guyon was harming the order of the school by her teaching. On May 2, 1693, Madame de Maintenon issued a command that Madame Guyon could not visit Saint-Cyr again. Guyon submitted to this order.

Madame de Maintenon then made an indirect plan to accomplish Guyon's destruction. Bishop Godet spread rumors about the dangerous Quietist influence at the school and Madame de Maintenon began to ask for Guyon's incarceration.

The crucial decision was then made by Guyon and Fénelon at this point to invite the intervention of the powerful Jacques Bossuet, Bishop of Meaux. They believed that he was a good man who would help them and save Guyon from another incarceration. A pious member of the French court brought Bishop Bossuet to Guyon's home, and Guyon openly gave Bossuet everything she had ever written without censoring it. Bossuet carefully studied all of these documents, but instead of being sympathetic to Guyon, he reacted in horror after reading her thoughts. Bishop Bossuet also began to seek the condemnation of Madame Guyon's theology.

One particular item that Bossuet objected to was contained in Guyon's *Autobiography*, where she wrote about the figure of the woman in Revelation 12, saying that she was the woman who was "pregnant of a fruit, which was that spirit you wished to communicate to all my children."(31) Bossuet expressed revulsion at such thoughts, saying, "My stomach was turned again and again as I read the teaching in her book."20

Who was this bishop who fervently pursued Guyon's condemnation? Bishop Bossuet had enjoyed great fame after his eloquent funeral oration in 1670 for Henrietta, the duchess of Orléans, who was married to the only brother of Louis XIV. Henrietta died an inexplicable, painful death in her early thirties from what was thought to be poisoning. Bossuet started the oration with a tribute to Henrietta's royal English lineage, saying, "Wherever I cast my view I am surrounded and dazzled with the splendour which streams from the crowns of England and of Scotland."21 Following this, he dramatically began to draw moral implications from her horrific death.

> Have we not seen the great and exalted of this world fall frequent sacrifices at the altar of God's vengeance for our instruction? And surely, if we stand in need of the impressions and terror to disenchant us from our attachment to the world, the calamity with which we are now subdued, is sufficiently awful! Oh ever memorable! Oh disastrous, oh terrific night! When consternation reigned throughout the palace! When, like a burst of thunder, a desolating voice cried out, Henrietta is expiring, Henrietta is no more!(188)

Bossuet pleaded with the French aristocracy to learn a lesson about the dangers of trusting in the power of the royal station.

> If persuasion hung upon my lips, how earnestly would I entreat you to begin from this hour to despise the smiles of fortunes, and the favours of this transitory world! And whenever you shall enter those August habitations, those sumptuous palaces, which received an additional luster from the personage we now lament; when you shall cast your eyes around those splendid apartments, and find their better ornament wanting! then remember that the exalted station she held, that the accomplishments and attractions she was known to possess, augmented the dangers to which she was exposed in this world, and now form the subject of a rigorous investigation in the other.(191)

In the funeral oration of Henrietta, duchess of Orleans, Bossuet employs the image of every human life being like a river flowing to the ocean. When a life reaches the ocean at death, Bossuet says, "honours, distinctions, and worldly prerogatives are unacknowledged and unknown; like rivers which lose their name and their celerity when they mingle with the ocean."(185-186) This metaphor emphasized that royal favors passed away as the person died and journeyed into the eternal presence, leaving the person alone with God.

Bossuet acted as a confidant to King Louis XIV and exerted tremendous influence in France. The powerful Bishop energetically strove for the continued power of the Roman Catholic Church in a land torn apart by religious strife, jealously defending the church against what he perceived as threats from nonconforming Catholics, Protestants, and freethinkers. He wrote against the burgeoning Enlightenment philosophy.

Bishop Bossuet also spoke strong words against King Louis XIV's building and plans for establishing the court at Versailles. Bossuet called Versailles the City of the Rich and said that no one need attack this court because the seeds of its destruction were in its faulty conception.

Bossuet had chosen Fénelon as a protégé. Bossuet fervently worked to get Guyon declared a heretic and, when Fénelon defended Guyon in his writing of *Maxims of the Saints*, Bossuet turned his power against his former student.

Who was this powerful woman Madame de Maintenon? She lived an extraordinary life, rising from a poor, orphaned teenager to the wife of King Louis XIV. She was born in 1635 as Françoise d'Aubigne into a noble, Protestant family whose penniless father took them to the island of Martinique that the French had recently colonized. He died upon arrival there, leaving his family in dire straits. Françoise's mother rejected her daughter emotionally and frequently physically beat her. They managed to get back to France, whereupon the mother also died. At the age of sixteen, now a frightened orphan, Françoise converted to Catholicism, starting her long ascent into the heart of the royal court. She married an older, crippled artist, Monsieur Scarron, who died when she was only twenty-five. Once again, she had to find a way to support herself. She received an offer from the mistress of Louis XIV, the Marquise de Montespan, to care for their children. Madame Scarron took this job, and started to ingratiate herself with Louis by her obvious devotion to his children. Eventually the king cast away the Marquise de Montespan and became enamored with the nanny, Madame Scarron. King Louis proposed marriage to her and they were secretly wed in the presence of only three witnesses. This morganatic marriage was kept secret their entire life, a fact that caused great consternation to Madame de Maintenon.

Both Bishop Bossuet and Madame de Maintenon enjoyed the favors of King Louis XIV. As the controversy over Quietism developed, Bishop Bossuet examined Guyon's writings for six months and then arranged for a meeting with Madame Guyon in January of 1694. Though he found her visions and theology troubling, Bossuet believed that Guyon was nonetheless a good Catholic. He gave her a certificate stating she was a genuine Catholic with an orthodox faith and served her the Eucharist at the time he did this.

Both Guyon and Fénelon fervently prayed that these accusations would now end, but they did not. Madame de Maintenon hoped that Guyon would be proven a heretic and that Fénelon himself would condemn Guyon.

The historian Duc de Saint-Simon stated that Maintenon became jealous of Guyon's spiritual insights. Also, Madame de Maintenon desired personal achievements including being named the Queen of France. These accomplishments were above her capabilities, and the resulting unhappiness caused her to despise Guyon's accomplishments.

Maintenon also desired more attention and respect from Archbishop Fénelon. Michael de la Bedoyere, a scholar of this controversy, speculates that Madame de Maintenon was "playing for Fénelon's spiritual favors."22 Fénelon had been critical of Madame de Maintenon saying, "Your ego, about which I have so often spoken to you, is still your unbroken idol."(93) Madame de Maintenon wished to end Fénelon's respect for Madame Guyon in hopes of gaining his regard.

Madame Guyon's relationship with Archbishop Fénelon complicated the heresy charges made against her by drawing into this situation a highly respected archbishop.

Guyon, a prolific letter writer, corresponded frequently with Archbishop Fénelon. The number and frequency of their letters were kept secret by various means, and although their opponents tried to use some of these letters against them, many remained hidden. On April 8th, 1689, Fénelon wrote to Guyon, "I do not know what you do to others, but you bring me many benefits. I would be delighted to be silent with you. I must see you before you leave, to speak of God and to be silent in Him at the home of (Mme de Maintenon). Arrange a day with her; she will inform me of it. Be sure that I speak to you with complete simplicity."23 When Guyon's Inquisition became fierce, Fénelon arose as her strong defender.

Throughout the course of their friendship, Fénelon believed that Guyon indeed did have a special relationship with God. He asked for her guidance in developing his own mystical sense and also turned to her for help with his own spiritual problems. But to whom could Fénelon turn to for wisdom and comfort in his strenuous life? Madame Guyon could nurture and care for Fénelon, which she did quite capably. Through letters, occasional meetings, and oral messages passed on by mutual friends, their contact had intense meaning for both of them. Fénelon found escape from his demanding life while Guyon believed that God used her gifts to care for Fénelon's soul. In his letters to Guyon, Fénelon says that she helped him escape from a dryness of soul and Guyon says that she found meaning in their rapport.

As they corresponded, Fénelon's career continued to rise. In 1687 he published his classic book *On the Education of Girls* in which he advocates giving girls a complete intellectual, spiritual, and practical education so they may be well prepared for their future responsibilities. The Duchess de Beauvilliers put his ideas into practice with her daughters, and the Duc de Beauvilliers requested that Fénelon be allowed to educate the next king of France. In 1689 Fénelon became the tutor for Louis XIV's grandson, the Duc de Bourgogne, giving Fénelon a powerful position in the court of Louis XIV. Guyon believed, as others did, that God would work a revival in the French court through the ministry of Fénelon. Other members of the French court, such as the Duc de Chevreuse and the Duc de Beauvilliers, also fervently sought a personal piety, according to Saint-Simon.24 They dreamed of a new and righteous France brought about through their prayers, beliefs and actions. This faithful group met regularly and became known as the Court Cenacle or Convent of the Court.

The Great Conflict Begins

Many persons looked beyond their personal concerns surrounding this case and recognized that what was at issue here was of grave importance. Fénelon and La Combe considered Guyon a genuine mystic, as did others, but because some such as Bishop Bossuet disagreed with their judgment of her, the issue became how to judge who was orthodox and who was not. Fénelon helped develop a plan in which trained theologians would directly address these issues. After careful study of mysticism, the desired outcome would be to clear up the unsubstantiated rumors about Guyon. Ultimately, it was the very essence of Christian spirituality that was at issue here.

A group consisting of Bossuet, Father Louis Tronson (a former teacher of Fénelon), and Louis-Antoine de Noailles, the Bishop of Chalons, convened to analyze carefully the theology of Madame Guyon. This group made its existence confidential so that Archbishop François de Harlay of Paris would not have to be notified about the group, since Harlay was neither respected as a theologian nor as a person of integrity. They met at Issy, a rural area south of Paris, from July, 1694, until March, 1695. Their secret meetings became known as the Issy Conferences.

Archbishop Harlay's reputation was one of worldliness and inappropriate enjoyment of his position, while Bossuet was known for a more sincere piety than Harlay. Fénelon wrote about Archbishop Harlay later in life calling him, "corrupt, scandalous, incorrigible, false, malicious, artful, an enemy of all virtue, one who makes all men of goodwill sad at heart."25 Guyon hoped to be cleared by Bossuet, but this appeal to Bossuet actually brought disaster to her. Guyon insulted Archbishop Harlay deeply by appealing to another bishop while living in Harlay's jurisdiction.

Archbishop Harlay became angered when he learned of these secret meetings going on in his diocese to which he had not been invited to participate, and requested a meeting with Guyon. Following the advice of Bossuet, however, Guyon refused to meet with Harlay. Consequently Harlay officially censured Guyon's books in his diocese and placed them on the Catholic Index of Prohibited Books.

In 1695 during the course of the Issy conferences, Fénelon was nominated by Louis XIV to be Archbishop of Cambrai. Fénelon was then added to the list of members of the Conferences. His expertise on orthodox mystical literature established him as an authority in the committee. Following their lengthy meetings, this group issued a document. Written in the form of a catechism of the church, this document also issued a list of condemned books that were adjudged to contain the Quietism heresy. Guyon was not explicitly condemned in these Issy Articles.

The Thirty-Four Articles of the Issy conference were published and widely circulated in 1695, after being signed by all participants in this lengthy series of meetings. Throughout these articles runs the theme of allowing freedom for all believers in their different modes of religious expressions, although these expressions are subject to the judgment of the episcopacy. For a "small number of chosen ones," though, this group graciously stated that they "leave them to the judgment of the Almighty," acknowledging that in Job is given an example of an unusual religious experience not understood by many.26 All of the acts of virtues, along with certain liturgical offerings such as the Lord's Prayer and the Apostle's Creed, were affirmed as Christian obligations, with the proviso that "all these acts are united in Charity alone."(219) The participants in the Issy Conference united behind these articles, with both Bishop Bossuet and Archbishop Fénelon signing them. Following this Madame Guyon assented to this peaceful agreement. "He (Bishop Bossuet) brought me the articles composed at Issi. I asked him the explanation of some passages, and I signed them."27 The controversy should have been settled at this point, with the pacific unity that reigned in these Thirty-Four Articles.

Guyon went to live in Bossuet's cathedral town of Meaux in the Visitation convent in the winter of 1695, seeking Bossuet's protection from Harlay. Maintenon pressured Bossuet into helping with her plans to destroy both Guyon and Fénelon. Sadly, Bossuet started to torment Guyon with actions and words witnessed by his nuns. He first had her agree to the Issy Conference articles, which Guyon supported. Then at unplanned meetings he showed up at her convent room, once accusing her of not believing in the incarnation and at another time accusing her of being a heretic. He threatened her with penalties if she did not agree to sign documents agreeing to his charges. Guyon refused to cooperate with him and started writing letters telling friends what was happening to her at the convent in Meaux. Guyon explains in her *Autobiography*, "But the Bishop of Meaux, who had promised Madame de Maintenon a condemnation, and who wished to make himself master of the business, raised so many difficulties, sometimes under one pretext, sometimes under another, that he found means of evading all I had asked, and letting nothing appear but what seemed good to him."(301)

Bossuet accosted Guyon for six months, during which time Fénelon started rising to her defense, even speaking to King Louis XIV about this situation. Finally Guyon asked Bossuet for permission to leave the convent to which he agreed. The Duchess of Mortemart accompanied Guyon out of the convent after she said a warm farewell to the nuns. Bossuet wrote in his account of the controversy, "She asked my permission to leave in order to go to the Eaux de Bourbon. After her submission, she was free."28 These details are important because almost immediately Bossuet regretted letting Guyon leave his domain. He spread stories that Guyon had left against her will and had jumped over the convent walls to accomplish this. Guyon writes, "Hardly had I arrived when the Bishop of Meaux repented having let me go out of his diocese. What made him change . . . is that when giving an account to Madame de Maintenon of the terms in which this affair was concluded, she let him know she was dissatisfied with the attestation he had given me."29

Guyon writes about Madame de Maintenon, saying, "that she did it from a good motive, in the false persuasion she possibly was under, that as she had some years previously assisted to save me from oppression, she was bound to exert herself to crush me."(282)

The state now had an excuse to pursue Guyon. Bossuet asserted that Guyon was a dangerous criminal who had fled from both his examination and the justice that he offered. The police now hunted Guyon as if she were a criminal.

Guyon struggled to respond to this situation. She received advice from friends to leave the country and to hide herself from the Inquisition. She rejected the idea of fleeing the country. She did, however, hide herself from Bishop Bossuet for six months, living in Paris under assumed names from July 9, 1695, until her arrest on December 27, 1695.

How had Quietism become a national crisis in seventeenth century France? Bishop Bossuet accused Guyon of Quietism, saying she was influenced by Miguel Molinos, and because of this had become a dangerous person. Because of the seriousness of this charge, Guyon and Fénelon could suffer grave consequences, including capital punishment.

One reason for Bossuet's change of heart was that he desired to be named the Archbishop of Paris, an honor that he was ultimately denied. Bishop Bossuet hoped to gain favor with Madame de Maintenon by obtaining this condemnation, and thereby improving his chances for becoming Archbishop of Paris. Because Fénelon was also in consideration for this archbishopric, Madame Guyon believed that Bossuet provoked much of this controversy with her in order to harm Archbishop Fénelon whom Bossuet thought of as a competitor. Guyon wrote in her *Autobiography* about Bossuet's ambitions, saying "that he was building a lofty fortune upon persecuting me" and that Bossuet "aimed at a person far above me" who was Archbishop Fénelon.(321)

When charges were made against Guyon, she declared that she had never heard of Molinos. She also stated that she had never read his works but that she was influenced by St. Francis de Sales. Her inquisitors believed that Guyon had read Molinos' *The Spiritual Guide* and was writing his thoughts in her books. Guyon argued in return that this accusation was unfounded, saying that she actually needed to be educated about Molinos and Quietism.

By placing Guyon in the orbit of an already defined and current heresy, her condemnation would be more easily accomplished. Statements were taken out of context in her writings that exaggerate her passivity to the world and to God. Guyon complained that these charges were unfair, citing instead other statements that would balance out her position.

Bossuet based his charge of heresies on certain passages in Guyon's books. The most controversial of her books was *A Short and Easy Method of Prayer* that had been published in 1685. In this book Guyon describes the spiritual process of recollection that leads to an intimate experience of the presence of God. She advocates teaching illiterates how to pray and how the use of prayer can ease the pain of unhappy situations. Guyon advocated a total abandonment to God, saying that the believer loses his or her own will, "in the will of God; by renouncing every particular inclination as soon as it arises . . . by being resigned in all things."30 This resignation to God leads to strong and capable actions in the world. Guyon uses prayer and an interior life as powerful tools in fighting the harsh realities of life.

Another major source of controversy was Guyon's *Commentary on the Song of Songs*. In this commentary Guyon describes her relationship with God as analogous to having union with a human lover. Using the Song of Solomon, Guyon describes God as a pursued and pursuing lover who allures her with his prolonged absence. She says that her love for God has wounded her and she can find no satisfaction except with God. She begins a passionate quest to find God. Through this search, her own will becomes annihilated. Then, Guyon writes, God fulfills her and makes the divine will the only force in her life. Guyon believed that through the intense pain of this absence and joyous reunion with God, she found an abiding union with God.

The conflict enveloped those involved. Bishop Bossuet argued both against a passive, resigned attitude and the idea that human beings may find union with God, while Archbishop Fénelon stated that a few saints had experienced this spiritual growth. Both Archbishop Fénelon and Bishop Bossuet wrote voluminously about the theology of Quietism while attacking each other's position. King Louis XIV angrily confronted Madame de Maintenon and blamed her for these problems, as she attacked the reputation of Madame Guyon. A long and angry controversy about Quietism had arisen in this era of the Sun King.

Guyon's Major Works

Madame Guyon believed that her own books were given to her as a divine favor, and acknowledged the influence that the books written by saints exercised over her. In particular, Guyon mentions Francis de Sales, Madame de Chantal, Thomas à Kempis, Teresa of Avila, and John of the Cross as primary influences on her own theology.

In Madame Guyon's *Autobiography* she offers one primary metaphor to explain the sufferings and unhappiness of her life. Guyon states that she experiences a spiritual annihilation directed by God and calls this the crucifying operations of God. Guyon's intention with her *Autobiography* was to show how God gave her these experiences of a personal annihilation, not only for her personal redemption but also for the redemption of others.

Guyon believes that the predominant influence in her life was her intense love of God. In her *Autobiography* she writes, "I loved him, and I burned with his fire because I loved him, and I loved him in such a way that I could love only him, but in loving him I had no motive save himself."31

In *Spiritual Torrents* she writes about the Holy Spirit using the metaphor of a water torrent for the Spirit-filled life. She says that God is like an ocean with rivers traveling towards this ocean. The rivers each have different paths, some meandering and others rolling along at a steady pace. Still others carry large boats loaded with property, while other rivers dry up and die. But the best river gushes along quickly as a torrent does, heading quickly for the ocean. Nothing slows down or stops this torrent until it loses itself in the immense ocean. As the waters spill together, the river can no longer be differentiated from the ocean. Guyon believes that the torrent symbolizes how Christians should seek God. The Holy Spirit opens hearts to seek God passionately just as a water torrent pushes aside everything in its way until it reaches the ocean.

In Guyon's controversial book *A Short and Easy Method of Prayer*, she reveals her method of prayer that allows everyone free access to the Holy Spirit. Guyon describes a process of coming before the Lord in quietness and waiting to hear the word of God within the soul. In this process grace pours deeply in the believer's life and helps direct every decision.

In *A Short and Easy Method of Prayer* Guyon addresses words of encouragement to the illiterates in society. She says that those who are not blessed with intellectual gifts or those who have not had the privilege of an education may still reach God. In fact, she believed that special spiritual favors grace the lives of those who were illiterate. She states,

> Come ye dull, ignorant, and illiterate, ye who think yourselves the most incapable of prayer! Ye are more peculiarly called and adapted thereto. Let all without exception come, for Jesus Christ hath called all. Yet let not those come, who are without a heart; they are not asked; for there must be a heart, that there may be love. But who is without a heart? O come, then, give this heart to God; and here learn how to make the donation. All who are desirous of prayer, may easily pray, enabled by those ordinary graces and gifts of the Holy Spirit which are common to all men. . . .
> You must then learn a species of prayer, which may be exercised at all times; which doth not obstruct outward employments; and which may be equally practised by princes, kings, prelates, priests and magistrates, soldiers and children, tradesmen, labourers, women and sick persons. 32

Through prayer, all persons came into God's presence. Guyon supports even the outcasts of society in seeking a passionate relationship with God.

Beyond writing books on the spiritual life, Guyon interpreted the Bible's historical stories as metaphors for the interior journey. Guyon believed that the Christian should work towards perfection by looking inside and confronting the sin and corruption in the human personality. Once the sin was uprooted, divine graces grow fresh, interior roots.

In *Commentary on Genesis* she describes the spiritual process of annihilation that the Holy Spirit forms and accomplishes in a believer's life. For example, in Genesis 1:1 we read "God created the heavens and the earth." Guyon interprets this to mean that the person goes through an interior and exterior renewal. The Holy Spirit moves lovingly through the person's life and creates a new, innocent soul. Another example of her interpretation of Biblical stories metaphorically is the story of the patriarch Joseph being sold into slavery. Guyon interprets this as an example of all the troubles that interior Christians suffer because the world does not understand the ways of living an interior life, which is a life lived allowing God to move deeply into the person's heart.

In Guyon's commentary on *Revelation*, she writes a theology of the church that states that the church is beginning a new era. In this new age, the church reacts to a new infusion of the Holy Spirit. Because of this changing understanding of the Holy Spirit, the church will flourish under the inspiration of new, Spirit-directed leaders. The Holy Spirit guides the direction of this change that leads to new discoveries about the potential powers of interior Christians.

Guyon in her *Commentary on Job* says that the story of Job is the story of every interior Christian. The sufferings that Job undergoes are a metaphor for the life of the interior Christian. Guyon's thesis is that only the most innocent of people suffer trials as did Job. She writes that Job "shows . . . that trials are the surest sign of innocence, and because a person is pleasing to God—— as the Angel said to Tobit."33

Guyon also offers many, vivid metaphors in her poetry about the work of the Holy Spirit. One of her major poems is named "A Figurative Description of the Procedure of Divine Love. In Bringing a Soul to the Point of Self-Renunciation and Absolute Acquiescence."34 In this poem Love calls her to join him in the ocean. She joyfully responds to this invitation to join Divine Love. At first vessels help her out into the ocean to find this Love, and then the boats leave her alone with little support except floating rushes. But even after this disaster, she does not resent Love but waits patiently. Then even these small supports such as floating plants disappear and she waits for death as the water tumbles over her. At this point she tells Love that whatever he wants for her is good and she consents to his will. That is what Love wants, she says, because after this acquiescence, Love returns to her. They are now united as bridegroom and bride. In the title of this poem, Guyon acknowledges her use of figurative speech or metaphor.

In her poem "A Child of God Longing to See Him Beloved" Guyon writes of her tremendous sorrow of heart. She says that the impious age in which she lives brings her sorrow and grief. She writes,

> I fly to scenes romantic;
> Where never men resort;
> For in an age so frantic
> Impiety is sport.
> For riot and confusion
> They barter things above;
> Condemning, as delusion,
> The joy of perfect love.(20)

Even in this impious age, she says, Providence cares for her and protects her from vain men. She experiences life as if she were a child playing peacefully under the care of divine Providence. An important part of Guyon's thought is her belief in the importance of child-like faith that comes through the work of the Spirit.

In the poem "Aspirations of the Soul after God" Guyon creates a metaphor for God's will, saying that it is a treasure. "My Spouse! In whose presence I live, Sole object of all my desires. . . . Thy will is the treasure I seek."(22)

In her poem "Self-Love and Truth Incompatible" Guyon describes a monster coming from the wilds. The monster is so ugly that birds fall at the sight of him and stop flying. Fear and terror arise at the sight of the monster. But a sage comes and addresses the person saying that this terror will cease if she will surrender her heart to God. Once a heart is surrendered, then this dreadful waste will bloom again and joy will come. Guyon then states in the poem that the dreadful monster is self-love. Self-love and truth cannot live together in one heart, Guyon asserts.

Guyon includes many of her spiritual themes in a poem entitled "Love Increased by Suffering." She writes of the joys of pure love in the heart. This love overpowers the horrors of prisons and human cruelty.

> The God of our desires;
> Tis there he stamps the yielding mind,
> And doubles all its fires
> Flames of encircling love invest,
> And pierce it sweetly through
> Tis fill'd with sacred joy, yet press'd
> With sacred sorrow too.
> Ah love! My heart is in the right—
> Amidst a thousand woes.(82-83)

Guyon's most common metaphors in her poems are ones taken from wild and untamed nature. Among these metaphors are monsters, mountains, stars, moons, torrents, and fountains. An example of this is from the poem "The Secrets of Divine Love are to be Kept." Each stanza starts off with an address to another part of nature. For one example, she writes, "Ye deserts! Where the wild beasts rove, Scenes sacred to my hours of love."(55)

In her commentary on *Song of Songs* Guyon writes of the passionate love relationship between the soul and God known as the bridegroom. Guyon draws the image of a relationship with God, using the metaphor of an intense, love relationship for the one between the Holy Spirit and a trusting believer. Guyon says that the kiss is the symbol for essential union between God and the believer. "Let him kiss me with the kisses of his mouth, for thy love is better than wine," she quotes from the Song of Solomon 1:1. She writes about God the Bridegroom, "Sensible grace, which is here signified by the name of the Bridegroom, penetrates the whole soul so powerfully with the sweetness which God sends to the souls He intends to fill with His love, that it is truly like balm poured forth, which extends and insensibly increases, in proportion as it is more and more poured out, and with so excellent an odor that the young soul finds itself wholly penetrated by its power and sweetness."35 This fragrant balm "gives rise to the prayer of recollection; because the senses as well as the powers all run after its odor, which causes them to taste with delight that the Lord is good."(31)

The believer yearns for consummation with the Bridegroom. "O Thou, whom I love so much the more as I find my love more thwarted; ah, show me where Thou feedest Thy flocks, and with what food Thou satisfiest the souls that are so blessed as to be under Thy care!"(36) For long periods of time the Bridegroom disappears and the lover pines with longing. During this separation the believer changes from self-possession into moving into the very being of God. This adventuresome path requires great endurance during this time of confusion as the believer away from self-appropriation into the union with the Bridegroom.

The union occurs when the bride has moved entirely outside of herself. She expresses her joy at the pleasure of union, "*I am my Beloved's, and my Beloved is mine!* O wonderful gain! I can describe it no farther than that I am unreservedly given up to my Beloved, and that I possess him without obstacle, hindrance or restraint! O, worthy to be envied of the angels! . . . Thou art so fully thy Beloved's that nothing hinders thee from being lost in Him; since thou has been wholly melted by thy heat of his love, thou hast been ready to be poured into Him as into thy final End."(98)

Guyon writes about the experience of the marriage between the soul and God. "The Bride invites the *Holy Spirit*, the Spirit of life, to come and breathe through her, in order that this garden, thus filled with flowers and fruits, may put forth its spicy perfumes for the help of souls. The Bridegroom, too, requires that the resurrection of his Spouse may be hastened, and that she may receive new life by the in-breathing of that life-giving soul, to the end that the marriage may be perfectly consummated."36 Realizing how unusual this sounds, Guyon writes, "This is far from imaginary, as will be attested by every person of experience."37

Guyon explains that this spiritual process works because of the character of the human heart. She writes about the innate love of God that dwells in the human heart. Through prayer the person remembers the presence of God without the constraints of time. This Platonic idea called recollection plays an important role in the theology of both Guyon and Fénelon.

> Therefore God at that time, communicated to man, a desire, a capacity to enjoy him as his only good, by sowing into him a seed of the woman, a spark of life, an instinct of goodness, a taste of heaven, a principle of holiness, a touch of love, the pearl of the gospel, the pledge of immortality, the hidden kingdom of God——All which expressions, are insufficient to express that inward treasure of the soul, which God in the beginning of the redemption, or as his act of redemption, communicated to man.
>
> And in this degree of redemption is every creature that is born of Adam; he has this kingdom of God in the soul, as a grain of mustard seed, a spark of life, a pledge of immortality, and attraction to God: If he tramples this pearl under his feet; then his destruction is from himself; but if he will co-operate with that inward Redeemer which God has put into his soul, if he will suffer his spark to kindle, his instinct of goodness spread itself, the light of life to arise in him, the voice of God to be heard in him; then will the divine life, be brought forth in him; and when his body dies, he will fall into all the fulness of God.38

Madame Guyon explains her most powerful influences as the Bible and the writings of Francis de Sales. That may be seen as Francis de Sales writes at length about the annihilation of the person and says that from this annihilation will flow the experience of God's presence.

> Holy love takes up its abode in the soul's highest and most exalted region. There it offers sacrifices and holocausts to God, as Abraham did, and as our Lord sacrificed himself upon the summit of Mount Calvary. This is to the end that from so exalted a place it may be heard and obeyed by its people, namely, by all the faculties and affections of the soul, which it governs with an incomparable sweetness.39

Guyon, Fénelon and De Sales are all influenced by Plato's idea of recollection. Plato writes about recollection in the dialogue between Socrates and Meno. Socrates states that truths are written in the immortal soul and in the experience of recollection truth may be realized.

> They [priests and priestesses] say that the soul of man is immortal. At one time it comes to an end——that which is called death—— and at another time is born again, but is never finally exterminated. On these grounds a man must live all his days as righteously as possible. . . .
> Thus the soul, since it is immortal and has been born many times, and has seen all things both here and in the other world, has learned everything that is. So we need not be surprised if it can recall the knowledge of virtue or anything else which, as we see, it once possessed. All nature is akin, and the soul has learned everything, so that when a man has recalled a single piece of knowledge——*learned* it in ordinary language—— there is no reason why he should not find out all the rest, if he keeps a stout heart and does not grow weary of the search, for seeking and learning are in fact nothing but recollection.40

Plato recognizes that humans will criticize the process of recollection. Socrates says that when fresh recollections are "newly aroused" that have a "dreamlike quality." But with time, these dreamlike ideas become mature knowledge. (370)

Augustine also says that truths are written in the human heart and we remember these interior truths in the experience of recollection. These truths or ideas in the heart build an edifice in the mind. As example of this is the name of God in the heart that causes interior "deliberation born in your mind."41

As in Madame Guyon's theology, Augustine says that before the Fall of Adam and Eve, humans naturally enjoyed an interior intimacy with God. Following the Fall, humans became focused on external matters. After the work of the Holy Spirit, once again the human may enjoy interior intimacy with God.

Madame Guyon's idea of annihilation and sacrifice build both on Francis de Sales and Augustine's theology. This Augustinian theology helps influence both her interior life and distinctive theology of the Holy Spirit.

Chapter Two

Madame Guyon's Interior Life

Throughout the course of her life, Madame Guyon experienced numerous visions and dreams which revealed her place in God's kingdom and predicted what the future held for her and her allies in their fierce struggle with King Louis and the Inquisition. Guyon recognized the power of visions to guide the interior life and appropriated strength from their interpretation.

Guyon wrote about this spiritual gift being given to her, saying that she had the power of the "discernment of spirits, and the giving to each what was suitable to him."[42] She referred to her messages as "Oracles of Truth."[43]

Many scholars and religious leaders have wondered about Guyon, who she is, and how she used her spiritual gifts. Evelyn Underhill, author of *Mysticism*, considers her one of a category of "emotional mystics."[44] John Wesley, founder of Methodism, expressed some reservations about Guyon, saying that she was "far from judicious," that both she and Fénelon had "an amazing genius" but that her works were at times "exceedingly dangerous."[45] Who was this enigmatic woman, who suffered, loved deeply, wrote theology, and intervened on behalf of the poor?

Throughout Guyon's *Autobiography*, she too wonders who she is and puzzles deeply about the perplexing circumstances of her life. In her confrontations with Bishop Bossuet, she frequently asks him to show her the error of her ways. This attitude seems to be a sincere openness on Guyon's part as she seeks truth.

In her theology of the Holy Spirit Guyon stresses that the Christian interior life had differing levels of development. The highest form of Christian life she called naked faith while the lower form was the way of illumination. To stand nakedly in total openness before God was the summit of the Christian faith while the lower level of illumination contains visions and dreams that the Christian may experience. Guyon considers illuminations such as visions to be "good and true lights when they come from God."[46] She further declares that visions "are in the powers inferior to the will" and come from an angel of light "according to the power which is given him by God, causes the soul to see his representation."[47] These gifts should never be sought for directly because God alone should be the goal of every Christian, but God at times bestows these gifts for the sanctification of the believer.

Guyon participated in both of these levels simultaneously. Dreams and visions played an important role in her life. Through dreams, Guyon often received ideas of what the future held for her and her friends in this stormy controversy. In visions, she received new understandings of her spiritual identity and found strength to persevere in her long and protracted Inquisition.

Guyon acknowledges in her theology of the Holy Spirit that God sends illuminations to persons to help them in the difficulties of their lives but states that illuminations also bear some dangers. Guyon warns that dreams and visions may easily be misinterpreted, and because of this, incorrect understandings of the illuminations could lead many Christians astray. She felt that a too literal interpretation of dreams and visions could cause Christians grave misunderstandings. An example of this is when a friend of Guyon's dreamed that Guyon had many children, and this friend interpreted it to mean that Guyon would work with children. Guyon realized that the meaning of the dream was that her work would endure and she would have many spiritual children throughout the ages.48 On numerous times in her manuscripts Guyon also warns against making superficial and quick interpretations of illuminations, saying that only through the guidance of the Holy Spirit could true interpretations be made of visions and dreams.

Guyon explains her thought on illuminations and naked faith using the metaphors of dark and light. She says that illuminations are like bright lights given to us in the dark experience of life. To have an illumination is to have a distinct light about one's desired path in life. Through visions and dreams, the person knew the meaning of situations and what should happen next. Guyon states, though, that if the believer progresses in spiritual growth, these lights may be withdrawn, and the person would experience a darkness called "blind faith"49 which could be mistakenly interpreted as the displeasure of God.(70) This state is called the revelation of Jesus Christ to the soul, a "revelation which makes us become second Jesus Christs on earth through participation, and which brings to pass that he expresses himself in us."(72) In this "passive faith-infused light," faith becomes a general, indistinct light spread throughout the entire personality, including what Guyon refers to as the person's central depth.(80) This infused light cannot be seen by the person "because its excessive clearness prevents one from discerning or recognizing it."(79) Guyon offers the example that a distinct light of an illumination is like the light of a star, while the light of faith is like the light of the sun. The light of a star is more easily distinguished than the defused, general light of the sun.

As examples of those who had illuminations, Guyon offers the lives of the saints, saying that the church valued these persons who had brilliant gifts such as visions. Many canonized saints, according to Guyon, did not attain a high level of spiritual maturity but merely had gifts that dazzled those surrounding them. Guyon felt that this was a sign of the spiritual ignorance of many church leaders.

Guyon also writes about the gift of discernment of spirits. She defines this gift as understanding in persons the "character of their sanctity; those who have been more annihilated, or those whom God has sanctified by action."(204) When other persons approached Guyon, she states that sometimes she could discern the state of their soul and discern their truthfulness. This gift aided her defense during her incarcerations and interrogations.

Let us now turn to the interior life of Madame Guyon to see the interaction between her interior life and historical events.

Visionary Experiences

Madame Guyon loved her faith as a young girl and wanted to be a nun. These intense hopes were disappointed when her father arranged a marriage for her. After the trauma of this marriage and the abuse she suffered in it, Madame Guyon grew increasingly distressed.

When she was nineteen at the invitation of her father, the despairing Madame Guyon talked about her life situation with a monk who had recently come out of seclusion. She experiences her moment of spiritual enlightenment in this conversation.

> He hardly advanced, and was a long time without being able to speak to me. I knew not to what to attribute his silence. I continued to speak to him, and to tell him in a few words my difficulties about prayer. He answered me at once: 'It is, Madame, because you seek outside what you have within. Accustom yourself to seek God in your heart, and you will find him there." On finishing these words, he left me. The next morning he was very greatly astonished when I went to see him, and when I told him the effect his words had produced in my soul; for it is true they were for me like an arrow that pierced my heart through and through. I felt in that moment a very deep wound as delicious, as full of love, a wound so sweet, I desired never to be healed of it. Those words put into my heart what I was seeking so many years, or rather they made me discover what was there, and which I did not enjoy for want of knowing it. O my Lord, you were in my heart, and you asked from me only a simple turning inward to make me feel your presence. O Infinite Goodness, you were so near, and I went running here and there to look for you, and I did not find you. My life was miserable, and my happiness was within me. I was in poverty in the midst of riches, and I was dying of hunger near a table spread and a continual feast. O Beauty ancient and new, why have I known you so late? Alas! I was seeking you where you were not, and I did not seek you where you were. It was for want of understanding those words of your Gospel when you say, "The kingdom of God is not here or there, but the kingdom of God is within you.' I experienced it at once, since henceforth you were my King, and my heart was your kingdom, where you commanded as Sovereign, and where you carried out all your wills; for what you do in a soul when you come there as a King, is the same you did when you came into the world to be King of the Jews. 'It is written of me,' said that divine King, 'at the head of the book, that I will do your will.' It is what he writes at once on the entrance of the heart when he comes to reign.
>
> I told this worthy Father that I did not know what he had done to me; that my heart was quite changed; that God was there, and I had

no longer any trouble to find him; for from that moment I was given an experience of his presence in the central depth, not through thought or application of the mind, but as a thing one possesses really in a very sweet manner. I experienced those words of the spouse of the Canticles, "Your name is like oil poured out; therefore the young girls have loved you.' For I experienced in my soul an unction which, like a soothing balm, healed all my wounds, and which even spread itself so powerfully over my senses, that I could hardly open my mouth or my eyes. I did not sleep at all the whole of that night, because your love, O my God, was not only for me like a devouring fire, which kindled in my soul such a flame that it seemed bound to devour everything in an instant. I was all of a sudden so changed that I was no longer recognizable either by myself or by others. I no longer found either those faults or those dislikes. All appeared to me consumed like straw in a great fire.50

Madame Guyon's prayer life changes into one of happiness. In her prayer she finds the presence of God even while she still struggles with her difficult life.

Three years later Guyon receives a prophecy about her divine call in a spontaneous conversation with a poor man when she is walking towards the Cathedral of Notre Dame. The man tells Guyon that she is to achieve such a high degree of perfection in this life, that she will avoid purgatory, yet have much worldly suffering. This conversation marked a turning point in Guyon's life, deepening her seriousness about her religious search.

> I listened to him in silence and with respect, while those who followed me said I was conversing with a mad man. I well felt he was enlightened with the true wisdom. He told me, moreover, that God did not wish me to be content to work, like others, to secure my salvation by merely avoiding the pains of hell; but that he further wished me to arrive at such a perfection in this life, that I should avoid even those of purgatory.(108,109)

Shortly after this conversation at the age of twenty-two Madame Guyon enters a time of horrific suffering. Madame Guyon and her three children simultaneously suffer from smallpox. Her middle son dies. Her young daughter and eldest son survive this devastating disease, though in a weakened and scarred condition. Madame Guyon begins a time of great grief and suffering.

Two years later in July 1672, Madame Guyon understands from a dream that her father has died. She travels to her parent's home and finds her father already buried. She returns home and within two hours her beloved young daughter suddenly dies. Madame Guyon writes in love for this child, "It was my only daughter, a child as much loved as she was amiable. You had provided her, O my God, with so many graces, spiritual and corporal, that one must have been insensible not to love her. There was noticeable in her a quite extraordinary love for God. . . . I regarded her as my sole consolation on earth."(152,153)

Immediately following these devastating losses, Madame Guyon follows the direction of her spiritual guide, Mother Genevieve Granger, the prioress of the Benedictines. Mother Granger advises Guyon to marry the Child Jesus in a private ritual. On the Day of Mary Magdalen, July 22, 1672, Guyon follows this direction and later reaffirmed these vows annually.

> The eve of the Magdalen's Day of the same year, Mother Granger sent me——I know not by what inspiration——a little contract already drawn up. She told me to fast that day and to bestow some extraordinary alms, and next morning——the Magdalen's Day, to go and communicate with a ring on my finger, and when I returned home to go into my closet, where there was an image of the Holy Child Jesus in the arms of his holy mother, and to read my contract at his feet, sign it, and put my ring to it. The contract was this: 'I, NC, promise to take for my Spouse our Lord, the Child, and to give myself to him for spouse, though unworthy.' I asked of him, as dowry of my spiritual marriage, crosses, scorn, confusion, disgrace, and ignominy; and I prayed him to give me the grace to enter into his dispositions of littleness and annihilation, with something else. This I signed; after which I no longer regarded him but as my Divine Husband. Oh, how that day has been since for me a day of grace and of crosses! These words were at once put into my mind, that he would be to me 'a Husband of Blood.' Since that time he has taken me so powerfully for his own, that he has perfectly consecrated to himself my body and my spirit through the cross. (152,153)

In this action, Guyon places herself in the long-recognized tradition of devotion to the Child Jesus. This piety nurtures obedient abandonment to God's will and participation in a spiritual childhood. Many saints, particularly Teresa of Avila, also practiced abandonment to the Child Jesus. Devotion to the Child Jesus also calls for the literal care for children and nurturing in all persons the child-like qualities of spontaneity and joy. Much of Madame Guyon's subsequent ministry lived into these devotional ideals. Madame Guyon later writes a short book about this form of spirituality called *The Infancy of Jesus*.

Following this interior decision, Madame Guyon actively made food and fed the hungry peasants in her area of rural France. She made hundreds of meals a month as she attempted to meet their desperate needs.

Following this commitment Guyon experienced renewed vigor for her active work, despite her intense grief at the deaths of many family members. Madame Guyon subsequently bore two more children. In 1674 she bore a son Jean-Baptiste-Denys and in 1676 a daughter Jeanne-Marie was born. When Jeanne-Marie was four months old, Madame Guyon's husband dies.

Madame Guyon begins to experience a call to minister in the area surrounding Geneva close to her spiritual friend, Father La Combe. In this dream Guyon peacefully receives a standard and a cross, while monks and priests attempt to stop the safe delivery of this to her. She says that she was for Calvary where Jesus was crucified, not Mount Tabor where Jesus experienced the wonders of the Transfiguration. She tells the following dream to a monk.

> I related to him even a dream that appeared supernatural, which had occurred to me on the night of the Transfiguration ... I seemed to see

> the ecclesiastic of our house with my youngest son, looking with much admiration at the heaven. They cried out, that the heaven was open. They begged me to come, that they saw Tabor and the heaven opened. I told them I did not wish to go there; that Tabor was not for me; that I needed only Calvary. They pressed me so strongly to go out that, unable to resist their importunity, I went. I saw only a remnant of light; and at the same time I saw descending from heaven a cross of immense size. I saw a number of people of all kinds—priests, monks—endeavouring to hinder it coming. I did nothing but remain quietly in my place, without trying to take it; but I was content. I perceived it approached me. With it there was a standard of the same colour as the cross. It came and cast itself of its own accord into my arms. I received it with extreme joy. The Benedictines having wished to take it from me, it withdrew from their hands to cast itself into mine.(225, 226)

In the following recollection Madame Guyon identifies herself with St. Peter, quoting the scripture that on this rock the church is built. Her spiritual director Father La Combe recognized and affirmed this vision, knowing that Guyon was a strong foundation upon which the church rested.

> After these words were put into my spirit, 'It is written of me that I will do your will,' I remembered that Father La Combe had told me to ask God what he desired of me in this country. My recollection was my request: immediately these words were put into my spirit with much quickness: 'Thou art Pierre, and on this stone I will establish my church; and as Pierre died on the cross, thou shalt die upon the cross.' I was convinced this was what God wished of me; but to understand its execution was what I took no trouble to know.... The following night I was awaked at the same hour and in the same manner as the previous night, and these words were put into my mind: 'Her foundations are in the holy mountains.' I was put into the same state, which lasted until four in the morning, but I did not know at all what this meant, paying no attention to it. The next day after Mass the Father told me that he had a very great certainty that I was a 'stone which God destined to be the foundation of a great edifice,' but he knew no more than I what the edifice was. (256,257)

At the time of Madame Guyon's call in 1680, King Louis XIV is in the midst of what is called the *Affair of the Poisons*. The woman who supplied chemical aphrodisiacs to Louis' mistress Madame de Montespan is arrested as a witch and tortured by the chief of police La Reynie. Louis struggles to keep this information about the aphrodisiacs from his country. La Reynie would later interrogate another woman in his keep, Madame Guyon.51

In 1682 Louis XIV moves his court to Versailles, a place he designed with hopes of Oriental splendor.

Madame Guyon's spiritual insights continue during this time in her life. A hermit tells Guyon this vision in which both she and Father La Combe are martyred and attired in white robes. Following their martyrdom, many persons drink from a spiritual well. Guyon and Father La Combe welcome their martyrdom, considering it an honor to sacrifice themselves for the glory of God.

> He once during his prayer, which was all in gifts and illuminations, saw me on my knees, clothed in a brown mantle, and my head was cut off, but immediately replaced; and then I was clothed in a very white robe, with a red mantle, and a crown of flowers was placed on my head. He saw Father La Combe cut into two pieces, which were soon reunited; and while in his hand he held a palm, he was stripped of his clothes, and reclothed in the white garment with the red mantle; after which he saw us both near a well, and that we were quenching the thirst of numberless people who came to us.(258)

When Madame Guyon travels with Father La Combe from 1681-1685, she uses her gift of discernment to understand their dangers. Guyon dreams frequently about Father La Combe and the sufferings that he goes through. In this dream she exercises prophetic gifts as she discerns what will happen to Father La Combe.

> A few days after my arrival at Gex at night I saw in a dream (but a mysterious dream, for I perfectly well distinguished it) Father La Combe fixed on a great cross of extraordinary height. He was naked in the way our Lord was pictured. I saw an amazing crowd who covered me with confusion and cast upon me the ignominy of his punishment. It seemed he suffered more pain than I, but I more reproaches than he. This surprised me the more, because, having seen him only once, I could not imagine what it meant. But I have indeed seen it accomplished.(285)

One of Guyon's friends dreams that Guyon will have many innocent children. Her friend misinterprets this to mean that Guyon works with children. Madame Guyon stated that the dream shows the numerous spiritual children she will bear.

> Before my arrival at Grenoble, the lady, my friend, saw in a dream that our Lord gave me an infinity of children; they were all children and small, clothed in the same way, bearing on their dresses the marks of their candour and innocence. She thought I was coming to take charge of the children of the Hospital, for the meaning was not given to her; but as soon as she related it to me, I understood it was not this; that our Lord by spiritual fecundity meant to give me a great number of children, that they would be my true children only by simplicity and candour, and that he would draw them through me into innocence.52

During this fruitful period of her life, Madame Guyon ministers to the suffering poor and writes in detail about reaching out to young girls who are in peril of entering the life of prostitution. Monks at this time were publicly beating persons, including priests, who used personal prayer and burning books that advocated prayer. In the following story Madame Guyon tells us of the difficult fate of a group of young girls who were trying to earn an honorable living while practicing prayer. Their group was broken up and they were driven away from the Church. But Madame Guyon sees hope in the fact that some monks delivered books advocating personal prayer, while others held public book burnings.

> There were also at Tonon girls who had withdrawn together into retirement; they were poor village girls, who in order the better to gain their subsistence and serve God, had several in number joined together. There was one who read from time to time, while the others worked; and they never went out without asking leave to go out from the senior. They made ribbons; they spun and gained a livelihood, each in her own trade: the strong supported the weak. These poor girls were separated, and others also, and dispersed among several villages; they drove them away from the Church. It was, then, monks of this same order of whom our Lord made use to establish prayer in I know not how many places, and they carried a hundred times more books on prayer into the places where they went than their brothers had burnt. God appears to me wonderful in these things. (69)

During this part of her life, Madame Guyon wrote many of her books including *Spiritual Torrents*, *Short and Easy Method of Prayer*, and her Biblical commentaries. As her *Short and Easy Method of Prayer* becomes more popular and her name becomes increasingly well known, Madame Guyon understands her danger from the Inquisition and enraged mobs of book-burning monks.

In another vision Guyon identifies herself spiritually with the woman of the Apocalypse who is bearing a child in a scene of great danger to both the mother and child. Guyon interprets this vision as a revelation of what she is accomplishing with her struggles as she bears the fruit of the spirit.

> One night that I was quite awake . . . you showed me, I say, under the figure of that woman in the Apocalypse, who has the moon under her feet, encircled with the sun, twelve stars, upon the head, who, being with child, cried in the pains of childbirth. You explained to me its mystery. You made me understand that the moon, which was under her feet, signified that my soul was above the vicissitude and inconstancy of events; that I was surrounded and penetrated by yourself; that the twelve stars were the fruits of this state, and the gifts with which it was honoured; that I was pregnant of a fruit, which was that spirit you wished me to communicate to all my children, whether in the manner I have mentioned, or by my writings; that the Devil was that terrible dragon who would use his efforts to devour the fruit, and cause horrible ravages through all the earth, but that you would preserve this fruit of which I was full in yourself, that it should not be lost——therefore have I confidence that, in spite of the tempest and the storm, all you have made me say or write will be preserved—that in the rage in which the Devil would be at not succeeding in the design he has conceived against this fruit, he would attack me, and would send a flood against me to swallow me up; that this flood would be that of calumny, which would be ready to sweep me away,

but the earth would open——that is to say, the calumny would little by little subside.(31-32)

While living in Turin, Guyon discovers that her search for an authentic life requires a courageous perseverance. Guyon writes of the courage necessary in life to meet the one she calls the Master. She crosses a stormy sea, ascends a mountain and comes to a locked door at which she knocked.

> Our Lord made me know in a dream that he called me to aid my neighbour. Of all the mysterious dreams I have had, there is none made more impression than this, or the unction of which has lasted longer. It seemed to me that, being with one of my friends, we were ascending a great mountain, at the bottom of which was a stormy sea, full of rocks, which had to be crossed before coming to the mountain. This mountain was quite covered with cypresses. When we had ascended it, we found at its top another mountain, surrounded with hedges, that had a locked door. We knocked at it; but my companion went down again, or remained at the door, for she did not enter with me. The Master came to open the door, which was immediately again shut. The Master was no other than the Bridegroom, who, having taken me by hand, led me into the wood of cedars. This mountain was called Mount Lebanon. In the wood was a room where the Bridegroom led me, and in the room two beds. I asked him for whom were those two beds. He answered me, There is one for my mother, and the other for you, my Bride. In this room there were animals fierce by nature, and hostile, who lived together in a wonderful manner——the cat played with the bird, and there were pheasants that came to caress me; the wolf and the lamb lived together. I remembered that prophecy of Isaiah, and the room that is spoken of in Canticles. Innocence and candour breathed from the whole place. I perceived in this room a boy of about twelve years of age. The Bridegroom said to him to go and see if there were any persons coming home from the shipwreck. His only duty was to go to the bottom of the mountain to discover if he could see any one. The Bridegroom, turning to me, said, "I have chosen you, my Bride, to bring here to you all who shall have courage enough to pass this terrible sea, and to be there shipwrecked." The boy came to say he did not see any one yet returned from the shipwreck. On that I woke up so penetrated by this dream that its unction remained with me many days.(54-55)

In the following dream Guyon foresees a rare gift to be given to her. She interprets this as a sign of her powerful ministry and possibly as a sign that she will have loyal friends, including that of Archbishop Fénelon. Faithful friends testify to her goodness in their brave actions: Archbishop Fénelon who destroyed a career for her and Father La Combe who suffered imprisonment rather than betraying Madame Guyon.

> I saw in a dream a number of beautiful birds that every one was eagerly hunting and desirous of catching, and I looked at them all without taking any part in it, and without wishing to catch them. I was

very much astonished to see them all come and give themselves up to me, without making any effort to have them. Among all those who gave themselves up to me, and which were numerous enough, was one of extraordinary beauty, which far surpassed all the others. Everybody was eager to catch that one; after having flown away from all, and from me as well as the others, he gave in, and gave himself up to me, when I did not expect it. . . . For two nights I had the same dream; but the beautiful bird which had no fellow is not unknown to me, although he is not yet come. Whether it be before or after my death that he gives himself entirely to God, I am assured that it will take place.(60)

During this time of Madame Guyon's life, King Louis XIV aggressively implements his policy of *un roi, une loi, une foi* ("one king, one law, one faith.") In 1685 King Louis XIV turned his state powers against the Quietists. He asked that the Vatican arrest as a dangerous heretic the Spanish priest Miguel de Molinos. The Vatican gave Louis this victory. Molinos was incarcerated on July 16, 1685, and endured a lengthy trial.

Louis XIV also began his aggressive action against Protestants. Louis issued his Revocation of the Edict of Nantes on October 16, 1685. This Edict of Nantes had promised protection to the Protestants in their worship. Now the Protestants could be arrested and killed for their form of worship. Approximately 200,000 Protestants fled France and about the same number were killed by French soldiers. Louis sent aggressive French troops called dragoons (the name is based on their dragon-like behavior) into Protestant areas to control them.

Bishop Bossuet approved of these actions to make all of France Roman Catholic through the Revocation of the Edict of Nantes. In protest of these actions, Fénelon wrote to Bossuet, "If they desire the people to abjure Christianity and to adopt the Koran, they need but to send them a troop of dragoons."53

Louis continued his push to religiously cleanse his kingdom of any religious belief but his own. On October 3, 1687, Father La Combe was arrested and began his life-long incarceration.

Louis XIV still was not satisfied and he continued to demand that Quietism be destroyed and the proponents of this religious attitude be incarcerated or killed. In 1687 the writings of Molinos de Miguel were condemned as heresy. Miguel began serving his life-long incarceration.

In 1688 Madame Guyon's books *Short and Easy Method of Prayer* and *Infancy of Jesus* were placed on the Index of Prohibited Books.

On January 29, 1688, Madame Guyon was arrested and incarcerated. While incarcerated, she understands that her suffering will be intense and long. In this dream while imprisoned Guyon experiences a religious state similar to Jesus in the Garden of Gethsemane. She believes that her destiny in life is to drink the cup of God's indignation and suffer as Jesus did in his life.

> For the day of St. Joseph, a saint with whom I am in a very intimate manner united, was as a day of Transfiguration for me. . . . yet on that day it was signified to me that I must enter upon new bitterness, and

drink to the dregs of the indignation of God. The dream that I had where all the indignation of God fell upon me came back to my mind, and I had to sacrifice myself anew. The evening of the Annunciation I was put into an agony I cannot express. The fury of God was entire, and my soul without any support from heaven or earth. It seemed to me that our Lord desired to make me experience something of his agony in the garden..54

After a time of intense suffering in her incarceration and separation without news about her young daughter, Madame Guyon was released on September 13, 1688, after the intervention of Madame de Maintenon.

Guyon frequently expresses profound introspection, in an attempt to understand herself. She tells of her experience as she left her first imprisonment in which she expresses poignant questions about who she is.

> Yesterday morning I was thinking. But who are you? what are you doing? what are you thinking? Are you alive, that you take no more interest in what affects you than if it did not affect you? I am greatly astonished at it, and I have to apply myself to know if I have a being, a life, a subsistence.(217)

In her *Mystical Sense of the Sacred Scriptures*, Madame Guyon writes with authority about the work of Jesus Christ who comes to reinstate life in its primal order. With its radical idea of Christ, this book later suffered a condemnation. Guyon believes that Jesus was to an example to all about how to live the Christian life. Guyon writes,

> Jesus Christ was not content to overturn these vain opinions of men by his words, he has done so much more by his example. He enhanced the nobleness of poverty by the choice that he made of it, and exposed the baseness of riches by the contempt he had for them. He showed that what men, deceived by their false imaginations call meanness was a veritable greatness, and that what they consider as something great, ought to be but the object of our scorn. In fine, in order to establish truth upon the earth, he found it necessary to overturn all things, or rather to reinstate them in their primal order, which lying and vanity had ruined.55

In 1693 Madame de Maintenon orders Madame Guyon never to return to her school at St. Cyr.

In 1693 François Fénelon is elected to be part of the prestigious French Academy.

In 1693-94 the Great Famine began. At least one tenth of the French population of about eighteen million people starved to death within the space of a few months.56

In about 1694 Fénelon writes his famous letter known as *Rémonstrances* to King Louis XIV in which he confronts King Louis about the many problems plaguing France. His letter is direct. "Thus it is that your people, whom you should love as your own children, are now dying of hunger. Cultivation is almost at a standstill, population in town and country is falling, trades of all kinds are dying out and producing ever fewer workmen; commerce is non-existent. Instead of extracting ever more money from your poor people, you ought to be giving it to them to buy food."57 In this letter Fénelon continues then to develop his just war theory, telling the king that wars may be fought for the security of the nation, but not to enhance the ego of the king. This direct confrontation addresses the fact that many of Louis' wars were designed to increase his fame and glory.

Madame Guyon continues her prolific writing. Madame Guyon states that through recollection she lived into the states of Mary, the mother of Jesus. In this unique Biblical interpretation, Madame Guyon asserts that Mary, the mother of Jesus, acted as the priest in the sacrifice of Jesus as she stood at the foot of the cross during the crucifixion. Mary had accepted the call from the angel to bear God's word and then served as priest during this holocaust of God's son. Guyon places Mary as priest in the tradition of the High Priest Melchizedek. This scriptural reference is from Genesis 14:18-20: "And Melchizedek king of Salem brought out bread and wine; he was priest of God Most High. And he blessed him and said, "Blessed be Abram by God Most High, maker of heaven and earth, and blessed be God Most High, who has delivered your enemies into your hands!" To place Mary as priest in the tradition of Melchizedek as priest is to connect her with the most powerful of priests in the Bible.

> Did not the angel ask the consent of Mary to be the mother of the Word? Did she not immolate him upon the cross, where she remained standing like a priest assisting at the sacrifice that the High Priest after the order of Melchizedek made of himself?(235,236)

Madame Guyon was arrested again on December 27, 1695. She began her incarceration at the Vincennes and suffered lengthy interrogations by the Chief of Police, La Reynie. These interrogations could legally have included torture; this was a common technique on women accused of being witches. On October 16, 1696, she was transferred to another prison at Vaugirard. On June 4, 1698, French authorities transported Madame Guyon to the Bastille.

In 1697 Archbishop Fénelon publishes his book *Maxims of the Saints* that defends mysticism as practiced by the saints. The book indirectly defends Madame Guyon's spiritual theology and became unpopular at Versailles because of the lofty ideals presented in the book.

Archbishop Fénelon's book *Telemachus* is published after a copyist gives the book to a printer in Holland. In *Telemachus*, Fénelon advocates that a king should serve his people through the actualization of pure love (also called disinterested love) in the political realm. With the application of pure love in the political realm, the king makes decisions that will benefit his people. This book becomes an instant classic and is published quickly in Holland, Belgium, Germany, England and France. King Louis XIV understands this as an indirect criticism of his kingship and takes great offense at *Telemachus*.

In August, 1699, Louis XIV experiences a mysterious visit from a country farrier who has seen a vision in the forest. This farrier was from the same town as Nostradamus who in the previous century had prophesied to the French royalty. The farrier describes the vision as, "a woman clothed all in white, but robed and crowned like a queen, very fair and shiningly beautiful."58 She identified herself to the farrier as the queen who had been the wife of the king. She gives the farrier a message for the king and gives the farrier information that only the king would understand. Louis talks with this farrier at length both in the presence of his ministers and in subsequent days holds two private conversations with this farrier.

King Louis later divulges that the farrier told him about the time twenty years earlier when Louis had seen a phantom in the forest at Saint-Germain and about which Louis had told no one. Louis spoke in praise of the farrier and granted him all expenses for his travel as well as a gratuity. The King also told the governor of his province to see that the farrier lacked nothing for the remainder of his life.

Saint-Simon in his historical memoirs states how unusual this event was and how no ministers of state would release what their conversations with the farrier contained. Neither would the farrier himself reveal the content of his message. The author La Beaumelle later connects Louis' experience with the phantom with the controversy over Quietism and believes that this is one reason Madame Guyon was eventually released from the Bastille.

In 1700 Bishop Bossuet calls for a reunion of the bishops from the Conference of Issy. At this meeting the bishops now clear the reputation of Madame Guyon by stating she has done no wrong.

Three years later Madame Guyon was released from the Bastille on March 24, 1703. Because of her broken health, she was carried out of prison on a litter.

Miguel de Molinos died in 1697 while incarcerated. Some believe that his death was an execution ordered by the Vatican.

How did Madame Guyon understand her role throughout this suffering? Madame Guyon used the role of mother in describing her spiritual ministry and addressed others as her children. At the end of her *Autobiography*, Guyon writes final words to her disciples saying,

> My children, I do not wish to mislead you, or not to mislead you. It is for God to enlighten you. . . . Oh, my children, open your eyes to the light of truth! Holy Father, sanctify them in your truth. I have told them your truth, since I have not spoken of myself. Your Divine Word has spoken to them by my mouth. He alone is the Truth. He has said to his Apostles, 'I sanctify myself for them.' Say the same thing to my children. Sanctify yourself in them and for them. . . . Holy Father, I have replaced in your hands those whom you have given me. Guard them in your truth, that falsehood may not approach them. . . . My children, receive this instruction from your mother, and it will procure life for you. Receive it through her, not as from her or hers, but as from God and God's. Amen, Jesus.(335, 336)

The similarities of this discourse to the farewell discourses of Jesus from the gospel of John in chapters 14-17 are striking. Guyon identifies herself as a mother responsible for other souls, praying for them as her life draws to a close.

The role Madame Guyon accepted was suffering from God as she pursued her active ministry. Guyon sympathized with those who suffered and could identify with weakness in other humans. Madame Guyon claimed to have experienced the ecstasy of the transcendence of God, while knowing the darkest human despair. She spent hours in contemplation of God, thinking on the scriptures, meditating on wisdom, and then offering her knowledge and insights to other persons. She taught illiterates how to pray, she taught beaten women how to endure what they could not change, and she spiritually fed priests, monks, and clergy of all stations in the Roman Catholic Church. She felt that she suffered because of the souls to which she was called to care and, in particular, she experienced suffering over her mediation for the soul of the incarcerated Father La Combe.

That Madame Guyon survived her Inquisition and was released is a great success, as compared to other Quietists who remained incarcerated and were executed. Father La Combe went trustingly into meetings with church authorities who were secretly planning his incarceration and was shocked by the results of the meetings. In direct contrast to Father La Combe, Madame Guyon prayed for and about each person and believed that she understood the intentions of each person towards her. She then acted accordingly to her perceptions. The fact that she survived her Inquisition, was eventually cleared of wrongdoing and released from the Bastille grants some evidence that she correctly understood her situation and acted with wisdom.

Chapter Three

Guyon's Theology of the Holy Spirit

What was the theology of Madame Guyon that catapulted her into an Inquisition and incarceration? Guyon develops a theology of the distinctive action of the Holy Spirit. She explains the Holy Spirit as "Love of the Father and of the Son, and thus the love with which God loves men; and He is the union of the Divine Persons, so He is the link that binds pure souls to Christ."59 Another definition of the Holy Spirit is "this Spirit (which is, which was, and which will be, the will and love of God communicated to men.)"60 Madame Guyon concluded that individual believers should give up a life of propriety and of self-interest, allowing the "crucifying operations of the divine spirit" to intervene. 61 The Spirit then creates the possibility for the person to reach beyond limits of personality to connect with others and with God.

Guyon's theology of the Holy Spirit as culled from all of her writings contains two main themes: pure love and annihilation. These two themes are descriptions of actions of the Holy Spirit or what Guyon calls God's "long, powerful and repeated operations."62 We will take these two main ideas consecutively.

Pure Love

Guyon devotes much of her theological writings to what she calls pure love and weaves this doctrine throughout all of her writings. She mentions it in her Biblical commentaries, in her *Autobiography*, and in her numerous books.

Guyon states "expression never equals experience" in talking about pure love. 63 To understand her use of the term pure love, one needs to look at both her thoughts and her descriptions of her states of mind. In *A Short and Easy Method of Prayer* Guyon says, "The language of love, though natural to the lover, is nonsense and barbarism to him that loveth not. The best way to learn the love of God is to love Him."(489)

What is pure love? In her commentary on the Book of Revelation Guyon writes, "Oh, pure love, divine exacting One, from Your omniscience nothing can be hidden."64 In this passage she uses pure love as a name for God, and that this pure love demands an account for our lives, an account so thorough that Guyon calls him the "exacting One." This exacting presence is omniscient; this overwhelming spirit sees and records everything that happens. God is the only source of both purity and of love found in this world. God's purity draws out our imperfections and, because of our corrupt nature, causes us to cry out begging for help with our troubled hearts. When we cry out, Guyon says, God listens, cares, and powerfully purifies our souls.

Throughout her documents Guyon attempts to describe the wonders of pure love. "Love, pure and holy, is a deathless fire" she writes. This reality is "love too vast for human thought" and is "ethereal fare." This "love overflowing" defies description and its beauty ravishes the receiver's heart.65

Guyon writes about her own experience of pure love in her *Autobiography*.

> I possessed God after a manner so pure and so immense, as nothing could equal. In regard to thoughts or desires, all was so clean, so naked, so lost in the divinity, that the soul had no selfish movement, however plausible or delicate; both the powers of the mind and the very senses being wonderfully purified.... The will, being perfectly dead to all its own appetites, was become void of every human inclination, both natural and spiritual, and only inclined of God whatever he pleased, and in whatever manner he pleased.66

Pure love involves an unmediated power that exists between a person and God. This warm love overflows from God to the believer and the person returns this feeling passionately to God. Guyon writes of the ecstasy of experiencing pure love.

> This new life is a settled state, wholly passive, without distinct or perceived lights of the soul, which, nevertheless, feels there a living principle, which moves, it, impels it, and which causes it to enjoy much deeper and purer pleasures than all it had enjoyed in its way of illuminations. It feels itself here united, bound and joined intimately to its God, in a manner as powerful as deep, without any sight, distinction or knowledge——without anything whatever: it is united, and that is all: it enjoys this union, which constitute all its life, and which gives it a distaste for all external acts, however holy they may be. Then it would not desire to do anything, except, like Mary, to love to remain in silence and repose. But, happy lover, what do you there? I do nothing, except that I enjoy a rest; and the more I delight in it the more it increases: I do not know what it is, except that it is all peace and rest.67

Pure love is an outpouring of the heart. In *Spiritual Torrents* the river that rampages towards the quiet ocean is a figure for the powerful force of pure love. The human heart experiences the love of God and passionately rushes towards this reality. Once the person connects with God, pure love becomes a teacher and a guide throughout the challenges of life. Pure love leads the person away from self-interest towards a holy union with God.

Guyon contrasts pure love with the lower spiritual level of having visions and insights, a process she calls illumination. Following illumination, the person may or may not move into the passive state of pure love.

The path of pure love was an option rarely taken in life, according to Guyon. Only strong souls found pure love. Guyon writes, "Pure love is only granted to a soul when, having come out of itself, it occupies itself with nothing but God; and this happens only *towards the evening*, in the latter period of life, and after great labours."68

Prayer is the medium for pure love, and through prayer, it opens the door to wonders and joys so potent that no earthly power could take them away. Even while imprisoned in the dungeon in the castle at Vincennes, Guyon wrote on the wonders she experienced through pure love.

> During the time I was at Vincennes and M. De la Reinie interrogated me, I continued in great peace, very content to pass my life there, if such was the will of God. I used to compose hymns, which the maid who served me learned by heart as fast as I composed them; and we used to sing your praise, O my God! I regarded myself as a little bird you were keeping in a cage for your pleasure, and who ought to sing to fulfill her condition of life. The stones of my tower seemed to me rubies: that is to say, I esteemed them more than all worldly magnificence. My joy was based on your love, O my God, and on the pleasure of being your captive; although I made these reflections only when composing hymns. The central depth of my heart was full of that joy which you give to those who love you, in the midst of the greatest crosses.69

Pure love was not only an abstract doctrine for Guyon. She lived her life based on it. This doctrine touched her emotions, thoughts, values and relationships. This thought about pure love also affected the people and world around her. Her influence on Archbishop Fénelon came primarily through her thought about pure love.

In her poem "Truth and Divine Love Rejected by the World," Guyon writes of the price of pure love. She believes that when a person loves purely, the world demands a heavy price from the person. She writes,

> The world is proud and cannot bear
> The scorn and calumny ye share
> The praise of men the mark they mean,
> They fly the place where ye are seen;
> Pure love, with scandal in the rear,
> Suits not the vain; it costs too dear.
>
> Then, let the price be what it may,
> Though poor, I am prepared to pay;
> Come shame, come sorrow; spite of tears,
> Weakness, and heart-oppressing fears;
> One soul, at last, shall not repine,
> To give you room; come, reign in mine! 70

The price of pure love is giving up self-interest. According to Guyon, a person experiences a reality called love that is not self-interested but a love that fervently clings to the love of God. This love requires an intense commitment to God and to the life God offers the individual. It purifies the person of self-love. God is to be loved beyond everything in life.

> If the manifold waters of afflictions, contradictions, miseries, poverty and distresses have not been able to quench the love of this soul, it is not to be supposed that the floods of abandonment to the Divine Providence could do it, for it is they that preserve it. If a man has had courage enough to abandon all the substances of his house and himself also that he may possess this pure love, which can only be acquired by the loss of all the rest, it is not to be believed that, after so generous an effort to acquire a good which he values above all other things, and which in truth is worth more than the whole universe, he will afterwards so underrate it as to return to what he had abandoned. It is not possible; God by this shows us the assuredness and persistence of this state, and how difficult it is for a soul who has reached it, ever to leave it again.71

How is pure love found in this world? Guyon states that pure love is found by living in an interior way where one focuses all of one's energies on God who lives within. The most explicit scriptural basis for this is from Luke 17:21 "The kingdom of heaven is within you." Because the focus for pure love is God within, it has only one fear which is the fear that "we will not please God enough or do His will."72

A central factor in pure love is the quality of disinterested engagement. Pure love changes the way the person perceives life and assesses situations. No longer will a person understand the situation according to self-interests, but purely to the interests of God. Guyon wrote, "So great is the indifference of this soul, that she cannot lean either to the side of enjoyment or deprivation. Death and life are equally acceptable; and although her love is incomparably stronger than it ever was before, she cannot, nevertheless, desire Paradise, because she remains in the hands of her Bridegroom, as among the things that are not."73

Annihilation

Annihilation is the second major theme in Guyon's books.
In her commentary on Revelation, Guyon explains the details of a complex struggle she calls personal annihilation, a struggle between pure love and self love whereby the former dominates the latter only with great difficulty. This battle, though, is not a cosmic struggle but the struggle of annihilation lies within every interior person. It goes through certain identifiable stages. In the first stage self-love is pushed out of the higher human faculties such as intelligence, reason, judgment, discernment, wisdom, strength, and deliberation or choice. After this struggle is fought successfully, then self-love can only live in the senses which Guyon calls the lower faculties. Guyon offers the metaphor that self-love first fails in the higher faculties and then is chased to the inferior part of the soul which she defines as the senses. While in the senses, self- love

causes confusion until pure love, still fighting for complete domination, vanquishes self-love from even the senses. This is what Guyon calls a personal annihilation.

The goal of the struggle involved with a personal annihilation is the deification of the person's soul. Guyon believes that as the person experiences increasing losses in this world, the soul becomes closer and closer to God. She writes in *Spiritual Torrents* that the believer possesses a "state of deification, in which all is God. . . . God does not divinize the soul all at once, but by little and little; and then, as has been said, He increases the capacity of the soul, which He can always deify more and more, since He is an unfathomable abyss."74

Guyon believes that only a very small number of people will engage in this struggle for many exert energy in order to avoid this intensity. Many church leaders themselves do not engage in personal annihilation, choosing instead to remain focused on human rituals and traditions rather than God within. They collude with their members in the practice of keeping their attentions externalized in the world about them. According to Guyon, the church brands the interior journey as a dangerous one, and that at times church leaders persecute those who try to follow the interior way.

Many also avoid the struggle because of the losses involved in the successful completion of it. Material wealth, personal honors, and acceptance by friends and family are frequently lost while the person fights for personal integrity of thought and life. Guyon bravely encourages others to continue in annihilation saying that worldly losses are not to be grieved over for the wonderful goal is to be living in God, the ultimate reality.

One experiences ecstasy upon successful completion of the struggle for personal annihilation. She writes,

> Oh righteousness of God, how cruel you are! You want only death. But how sweet and kind You are to this one who has no other interest than God's only, who has no more self interest, who being placed in this reality as an experience——worships, blesses and loves this apparent cruelty, given for so great a benefit. Your approach is rough and cruel, but your cruelty afterward changes into floods of delight. Oh, mystery of cruelty! Mystery of love and sweetness! Who will understand thee? . . . Oh Righteousness, whoever does not love You with the most extreme passion is not yet free from himself, though he may think he is. You are only in the hearts for which divine righteousness, in its most extreme severity, has only charms and sweetnesses. 75

The struggle commences with the ability to abandon oneself to the guidance of the Holy Spirit. This idea of abandonment for Guyon means to leave the propriety of the self behind in order to devote one's full energies to God. God calls chosen persons to abandon their self-interests and to love Him fully. To abandon oneself is to give one's very being first to God and then allow God to share his or her life. She writes in *A Short and Easy Method of Prayer*, "Abandonment is the casting off all selfish care, that we may be altogether at the Divine Disposal."76

The focus of energies is inwardly directed to God, not outwardly focused on the outside world. Guyon describes this abandonment as finding an inner kingdom of peace, joy and satisfaction. Guyon writes about the importance of this practice of abandonment for her life.

> I let others think what they please; for me, I find security only in abandoning myself to the Lord. All scripture is full of testimonies which demand this abandonment. 'Make over your trouble to the hand of the Lord: he will act himself. Abandon yourself to his conduct: and he will himself conduct your steps.' God has not meant to set snares for us in telling us this, and in teaching us not to premeditate our answers. When things were carried to the greatest extremity (I was then in the Bastille), and learned the defaming and horrible outcry against me, I said to you, my God, If you desire to render me a new spectacle to men and angels your holy will be done. All that I ask of you is that you save those who are yours, and do not permit them to separate themselves. Let not the powers, principalities, sword, etc., ever separate us from the love of God which is in Jesus Christ.[77]

Guyon uses spatial metaphors to describe the abandoned life. Abandonment means a going inside. The person lives within and then directs attention towards others. The person directs energies to God and to others but not towards his or her own self.

Guyon frequently refers to a personal annihilation as the martyrdom of the Holy Spirit. In her parlance, this meant that the believer does not direct or control the personal annihilation. The Holy Spirit initiates and develops the personal annihilation.

Guyon also understands the martyrdom of the Holy Spirit as the beginning of the third era in history. She says that historically in the times of the patriarchs and matriarchs there were martyrdoms for the Creator. In the early Christian era, martyrdoms for the Son occurred. In the third era, martyrdoms happen to allow the actions of the Holy Spirit.

The common objection to abandoning oneself to God within is that the person will no longer care about the external world. Guyon says that, to the contrary, by listening to God within the person is led to a deeper and more satisfying relationship with other persons and history. The concentration of the person's energy into interior life causes the person to care deeply about the world and its problems, because the person's powers such as intelligence and reason are carefully focused on the higher thoughts of God.

An example of this inner concentration and outer work is seen in Guyon's life in her trip to Geneva to care for the sick. She says that she placed all of her energies inside to her God and then felt what she calls a divine motion lead her to care for the poor and suffering. While Guyon developed an active ministry in caring for the sick, she concerned herself deeply with her daughter's well-being, and reactivated her friendship with Father La Combe. Her spiritual wisdom became known and many sought her for guidance. Madame Guyon, though, reiterates throughout her *Autobiography* that she focused all of her mental and spiritual energies on her interior God. As a by-product of this focus, she felt led throughout her days to live in an involved way with the world around her. Her theology asserts that when one abandons oneself to a pure, inner love, the person consequently lives in a responsible and caring way.

Guyon states in her theology that the human soul is divided into an inferior and a superior part. In the former resides what she understands as the sensible and animal nature while in the latter dwells the spiritual and divine nature of the human being. She believed that the first created humans received the righteousness of God in their spiritual and divine superior nature. In this God-given ordering the spiritual nature then directed the sensible and animal portion of their being.

After the Fall of humanity, the inferior senses consequently directed the spiritual, superior part of the human. Disorder now reigned, and because of this human beings needed a purification process that would take them back into the original order and innocence they possessed before the Fall. Annihilation fills the human need for a restoration of primordial order and innocence by once again giving the spiritual nature dominance over the animal nature.

As a metaphor of the experience of annihilation, Guyon interprets the story of Joshua taking the Ark of the Covenant (which represents the will of God) through the waters of the Jordan. As the Jordan River parted allowing the Israelites to pass through the river on dry land, the waters separated into higher and lower waters. This passage from Joshua 3:16 says, "The waters coming down from above stood and rose up in a heap far off, at Adam, the city that is beside Zarethan, and those flowing down toward the sea of the Arabah, the Salt Sea, were wholly cut off."

Guyon states that in the process of annihilation, God separates the inferior and superior part of the human in order to restore the human to an innocence that she defines as the will of God. This separation of the two parts is like the separation of the waters of the Jordan River when Joshua crossed.

> Then it is that the superior part remains in the purity of its creation; but the inferior finds itself, apparently, in all its malignancy, and without any relief whatever. It is even then, it seems, more malicious than it was when the superior part still communicated with it: for, although it transmitted its malign vapor to it, it still received from it some sweet influence; but here it is wholly abandoned with all its malignity, and suffers inexplicable anguish.78

In Madame Guyon's *Commentary on Job* she offers another example of personal annihilation. She interprets Job as suffering intensely in his natural state but still acknowledging God within his divine, superior part. In Job, she asserts, we see the total separation of his two natures as he goes through the process of annihilation. He suffers a malign, corrupt inferior nature while still acknowledging the divine and spiritual with his superior nature. The separation of these two parts causes great inner conflict. Both the divine natures and the malignant natures are highly developed, but because no commerce exists between the two, the malignant nature is without relief from the good influence of the divine nature. The person cries out for relief, as Job did, from the corruption in the lower nature.

Guyon uses two metaphors to describe the purification that God works in the inferior part. The first is that of a wine press into which God puts the inferior part of the soul and presses out the malignancy as grape juice is pressed from the grapes. In the second metaphor she describes the dirt gathered in a sponge. The Holy Spirit causes the separation of the soul, and the inferior part becomes more and more dirty. The inferior portion of the soul is like a dirty sponge from which God wrings out the dirt. Through temptations that are resisted, the person gains strength and primordial innocence is restored. This is similar to a sponge being twisted and wrung dry as the dirt comes out. After this painful purification process, Guyon writes that the "superior part is brought into the divine purity, and the inferior into the natural purity——both in complete innocence."(145)

Correction of the human disorder and restoration of the original order is accomplished through the process of annihilation. Following the painful cleansing that is likened to the wringing out of a dirty sponge, the person experiences a glorious restoration to a primordial, innocent existence. Guyon writes, "Then the inferior part receives a continual flowing from the superior without sending back anything: it is placed in the natural order of its creation; and it is the operation which leads to that which is called annihilation. All that belonged to Adam, the transgressor, being entirely destroyed, only the work of God remains."(146) Thus, the destruction of the malicious nature that humanity gained through the fall of Adam is the work of God done in the soul. This work cannot be accomplished by the believer but is the operation of the Holy Spirit called annihilation.

What awaits the person who experiences annihilation? The phrase that Guyon employs for this new life is "lost in God."(158) God and the individual person become one in a complete union.

Guyon states that extremely few persons find union with God. She describes this small number of annihilated persons as "being much more rare than we can believe." (146) After the annihilation the person becomes one with Christ, a union that includes participation both in Christ's sufferings and exaltation. Guyon writes in a letter, "Let all the world forsake me; my Lord, my Lover lives, and I live in him. This is the deep abyss where I hide myself in these many persecutions. O, abandonment! blessed abandonment! Happy the soul who lives no more in itself, but in God. What can separate my soul from God? Surely, none can pluck me from my Father's hands. All is well, when the soul is in union with him."79

As an example of annihilation that shows the restored life after its occurrence, Guyon offers her interpretation of Joseph in the *Commentary on Genesis*. Guyon says that Joseph is a "living expression of a predestined soul."80 At the beginning of his life he experienced spiritual graces and favors that delighted him along with dreams that promised him a bright future. But, after Joseph was sold into slavery, he experienced years of desolation. Guyon believes that this desolation happens to all chosen souls. She writes, "The sweetnesses of spiritual infancy are hardly passed than the strangest crosses are prepared. We see ourselves exposed to the most extreme persecutions."(356)

Following the extreme persecutions, an unusual path arrives, which God prepares for this predestined soul to rule in greatness, as Joseph did when he became the ruler of Egypt. Guyon believes other chosen souls become spiritual leaders with authority over souls. If the person opts for an obedient life, the destiny is worked through by the demanding, interior journey Guyon describes in her Biblical commentaries.

Why, though, does the interior person receive persecutions from the society in which he or she moves? Guyon believes that the persecutions are caused because the abandoned person's simplicity and innocence are mistaken for haughtiness. Guyon says that once the sense of propriety is lost, the person gains the reality of God's holiness, purity, and cleanliness. But others will attack these qualities in the abandoned soul, with accusations that they are not productive citizens. She states that simple souls are accused of being "*abominable and useless*; they accuse them of the vilest ungodliness, the forgetfulness in that state of themselves, and they say that *they drink iniquity like water*, on account of the immovableness of their conscience, which no longer existing, can no longer reproach them for anything: the source of iniquity being taken away, which is propriety——consequently the works of iniquity are done away."81

The question of why God desires the testing of the soul through the pain and humiliation of annihilation arises. Guyon states that this annihilation is necessary because the soul becomes stronger and purified through these strange trials. She felt that the annihilation was not only to be endured but the fruit of divine union was to be desired above all other experiences or states in life.

Guyon's theology of the Holy Spirit states that when the person has completed the arduous process of annihilation, he or she now stands responsibly before God. The believer follows the direction of the Holy Spirit and receives new spiritual powers to exercise on behalf of others.

Guyon writes that the vast majority of human beings need the compassion of a merciful God to overlook their sins. An extremely small number of persons are chosen to experience not the mercy of God but the justice of God. These persons who have allowed the Holy Spirit to destroy their selfish will, purify their hearts, and accept God's fiery justice in their lives are recipients of divine justice. Of them she writes:

> Shortly after I entered the convent I had a dream. I suddenly saw the heaven opened, and like a rain of golden fire which appeared to me to be, as it were, the fury of God, which sought to satisfy itself and do justice to itself. There were with me a great number of persons who all took to flight to avoid it. As for me, I did quite the contrary. I prostrated myself on the earth, and I said to our Lord, without speaking to him otherwise than in the manner he knows and understands: 'It is I, my God, am the victim of your divine justice; it is for me to endure all your thunderbolts.' Immediately all that rain, which was of flaming gold, fell upon me with such violence that it seemed to deprive me of life. I woke with a start, fully certain that our Lord did not desire to spare me, and that he would make me pay well for the title of 'victim of his justice.'82

Maintaining the Holy Spirit in a person's soul results in the longing for and acceptance of God's justice. Although persecutions are sometimes thought of as an expression of God's wrath or punishment for sins committed, Guyon believed that they are a sign of God's favor and pleasure. In this quote she develops these ideas.

> O, Divine Lover, who delightest Thyself only, it seems, with these loving cruelties, is it not enough to have wounded Thy lover in a thousand places, without coming again to throw it down, and in that way to give occasion to all its enemies to oppress it, to trample it under foot, and to reduce it to dust! Its enemies, in triumphing over it, will insult all Thy servants. No matter; I desire to have this soul treated in like manner, and that He may have no compassion upon it. *I have* done, said Job, what I could to hide my wounds from myself, *putting sackcloth upon my skin*, and appearing as though I did not see them: I am *humiliated* beneath the *dust* of my nothingness: *I have wept until* my eyes *have become swollen* and *dim*. All that has not appeased my Judge; on the contrary, it has still increased His severity. O Job, and you, children of men who are chosen to be the delight of God, you are the victims of Divine Justice: it is over you that it takes pleasure in exercising its power. Let sinners have compassion; but for you, take delight in being exposed to all the arrows of its fury, without its having pity upon you.
>
> Job causes us still to observe a truth, which is, that these states do not arise when a person has offended God, but when the soul is the most innocent, when it is more devoted to God and more united to Him; for these are not the tests of weak persons, but of those who are the strongest and the purest, and whose *prayer* is very sublime, *very pure* and open.83

Guyon offers the term holocaust to explain this experience of annihilation. Through divine love God takes the soul as a sacrifice offered to him. She writes in her *Autobiography* about this operation of the Holy Spirit. "This love delights in making those whom it has made one in you the continual victims of its justice. It seems that these souls are made holocausts to be burnt up by love on the altar of the divine Justice."84

After this personal sacrifice, the person becomes a spiritual leader. Guyon expresses in many of her books that her own innocent sufferings prepared her to become the spiritual mother of many, saying that her sufferings were used by God to nourish many other souls. In the final words in her *Commentary on Job* she writes,

> *Job*, after all these states of trial, *lived much longer* a life wholly divine; God giving to him a life as long and abundant, as his death had been severe and bitter, and his corruption terrible. God gave to him a *great posterity*: the souls that God presses forward so forcibly and so swiftly. He urges them onward in that way only to use them in helping and rendering service to others, and only to give them a great number *of children*. This holy race multiplies itself instantly: God wins souls by these souls, and those that they have won, win also an

infinite number of others for God, and that goes on multiplying greatly; so that a single soul can contribute to the perfection of a very great number of others.85

Guyon believes that the suffering of chosen souls, such as the patriarch Joseph and Father La Combe, redeems other human souls, by participating in the spiritual state of an apostle. Guyon describes this state in this way.

> Our Lord made me comprehend what the apostolic state was, with which he had honoured me; that to give one's self up to the help of souls, in the purity of his Spirit, was to expose one's self to the most cruel persecutions. These very words were imprinted on my heart: To resign ourselves to serve our neighbour is to sacrifice ourselves to a gibbet. Such as now proclaim, *Blessed is he who cometh in the Name of the Lord*, will soon cry out, *Take away, crucify*.86

The last portion of this quote calls into question the sufficiency of Christ's sufferings for the redemption of the human race. The source of this belief is Paul in Colossians 1:24 who wrote "Now I rejoice in my sufferings for your sake, and in my flesh I complete what is lacking in Christ's afflictions for the sake of his body, that is, the church."

The believer receives a special role in God's plan of salvation and has power to lead other souls closer to God. Guyon stated that the more dependent she became on God, the more she became a victim of the Holy Spirit, then, paradoxically, the more power she received over other souls. She writes,

> Thus the Spirit of God was so completely the master, that I had to do everything that pleased him. His will was not concealed from me; he led me from within like a child, while he rendered my whole exterior childlike.... Our Lord, however, with the weaknesses of his childhood gave me the power of a God over souls, so that with a word I cast them into trouble or peace, according as was necessary for the good of those souls.87

Guyon believed that special powers of communication existed between her and other souls over which she had authority. Such a relationship between her and a local friar existed, communicating with him through the bond that existed between their souls, utilizing no sensory faculties.88

> Our Lord gradually taught him to speak in silence, and to receive grace without the intervention of words; but this took effect in him only in proportion as he died to himself....
> In proportion as his soul advanced so as to be able to remain in silence before God, and the Word operated in him in this silence—which is fruitful and full, not a mere indolence, as those who have not experienced it imagine—he increased in grace and prayer. O immediate speech, ineffable speech, who say everything without articulating anything, who are the expression of what you say! He who has not experienced you knows nothing, however wise he may think him-

> self. In you is the source of all knowledge, and when you are in plenitude in a soul, what is she ignorant of? In proportion, then, as the Word communicated himself to him in silence ineffable, it was given him in silence to communicate with me, and to receive through me in silence the operations of the Divine Word—operations which he could not be ignorant of, for the plenitude became in him more abundant; like a sluice opened up which profusely discharges itself, and that with such force and such grace in well-disposed souls, that a river does not run with greater impetuosity. He was also given the means of aiding other souls, not in silence, but by words; for as to the communication in silence, those who are in a state to receive are not thereby in a state to communicate: there is a long road to travel before.89

Among Guyon's special powers was divinely dictated writing, where her mind did not engage as she wrote, but the words flowed in rapid succession as she wrote them down. She called this writing in a "purely divine" manner.(49)

Guyon describes operations of the Holy Spirit as mystic meaning "secret and imperceptible."90 The believer has a mystic death and the final outcome of this death is when "truly mystical souls, have no power of their own; all their strength is in God alone."(377) Guyon refers to these rare souls as "other Christs."91 She writes in her *Commentary on the Song of Solomon*.

> The souls of whom we now speak are other CHRISTS, which is the reason why we perceive in them less the features of the saints; but if we seek for the marks of the Lord Jesus we shall find them most clearly there.(105)

Once the union between God and the believer is consummated, little difference exists between God and the person. Guyon described the relationship between herself and God as "God is she and she is God."(101) The believer becomes one with the spirit when the process of divinization is complete.

Guyon weaves these ideas of pure love and annihilation throughout her books. Pure love guides the person through the process of annihilation, following which the person experiences a new, spiritual life. The believer receives new abilities and a place in God's plan of salvation. Guyon's theology of the Holy Spirit offers metaphors for how the Holy Spirit operates in the lives of a few, chosen believers. Her hope is that, "We must then allow the Spirit of God to act in us."92

Guyon's Implicit Theology

As we have seen, Guyon develops an explicit theology of the Holy Spirit in her writings but her actions reveal an implicit theology that she does not fully elucidate. In her refusal to follow the leadership of some church authorities, Guyon reveals a theology of the conscience and of the church that is not articulated directly, but provides an important foundation for her thought and actions.

Two reasons exist why we need to understand Guyon's implicit theology. First, this theology played a significant role in the church controversy as manifested by the reactions of both Bossuet and Fénelon. In her implicit theology, Guyon placed the importance of her own conscience above any directives from the leaders of either the church or the state. She said that God communicated to her through the intervention of the Holy Spirit and, because of this, she refused to change any of her actions even when King Louis XIV or Bishop Bossuet desired her to do so. Secondly, she shows evidence of a continuing struggle with her understanding of the Holy Spirit as shown by her actions, e.g. writing her own version of the traditional vows of poverty, chastity, and obedience.

Guyon placed a higher importance on following the guidance of her individual conscience than following that of church leaders. On many occasions she refused to follow the leadership of church officials when their advice conflicted with her conscience. Several examples of these conflicts exist in her *Autobiography* and in other histories. In one occurrence, church leaders asked Guyon to become a nun which she adamantly refused. Church leaders then offered to make her a mother superior without her going through the normal stages towards taking the nun's vows, a move she also spurned. She complained about what she considered the ridiculousness of offering her the office of mother superior, feeling that they were attempting to seduce her away from what God asked of her.93

Even though Guyon refused to take the traditional role of a nun, she claimed for herself the title of the bride of Christ, an action which church officials criticized. The Roman Catholic Church sometimes referred to nuns as spouses of Christ but the title was not used for lay persons. Guyon, however, had a dream that she became the bride of Christ, and made this fact public by writing about it in her *Autobiography*. She believed that church authority was not essential for declaring herself the bride of Christ; hence, she claimed it on her own authority.94

A great deal of ambiguity exists about Guyon's use of the title bride of Christ while refusing to become a nun. This title traditionally is used to describe nuns or the church in its entirety. For example, Francis de Sales referred to nuns as the spouses of Christ. The church also in its official documents refers to herself as the "Bride of Christ." Did Guyon think of herself as a holy woman who did not need to take religious vows in order to merit the term the "Bride of Christ" or did she believe that she participated in the beginning of a new church? Enough evidence exists in her writings to show her belief that the Holy Spirit was acting in new ways through her. In her commentary on Revelation, she writes of the new understandings of prophecies that will arrive in the future.

> This Holy Spirit comes from God to be outpoured on the creatures and Joel's prophetic word will be completely fulfilled. Although it was fulfilled when the Holy Spirit came on the whole Church through the assembled Apostles and the faithful, it was not however perfectly fulfilled, since this Holy Spirit was not out poured on all flesh, though it came on men and women. But a time will come when this prophecy will have its full extension.95

Guyon also asserts that a new beginning is coming to the church. She writes concerning the woman giving birth in Rev. 12:1-2, that the woman is the symbol of the new birth the church will have on this earth.

> The church is about to give birth to the inner spirit: her true spirit. She is with child, possessing this Spirit which is like a second advent of Jesus Christ. She is in pains to be delivered for it will cost her sufferings; the fruit will be precious and more good must be produced; suffering is, therefore, unquestionable.(80)

Guyon in her *Autobiography* identifies herself with this woman, a claim Bishop Bossuet challenged. An implicit theology emerges in Guyon that she understood herself as a new beginning in church history. In this new era, interior Christians would develop higher spiritual powers and lead organized religion into a new time of holiness both for the individual and for the church institution.

Guyon's understanding of the term bride of Christ is important for the development of a theology of the church. Since Guyon believed that this title was a gift from God, and that the church hierarchy did not wish for her to claim this title, therefore we can conclude that Guyon believed that the Holy Spirit did not need the church hierarchy to accomplish its work. We can further infer, as did Bossuet, that Guyon believed that the Holy Spirit could act in direct opposition to the church episcopacy, and that the Roman Catholic Church was not necessary for fulfilling the will of God.

Church officials attempted to chose a spiritual director unsympathetic to Guyon's theology in hopes of influencing her thinking; however, this effort was unsuccessful. Her spiritual director, Father La Combe, suffered persecution because he refused to command Madame Guyon to follow the directive of these church leaders. When the church took the drastic action of incarcerating him, Guyon wrote that La Combe was persecuted unfairly. She writes,

> I even made verses on it at the time; for truly it was given me to know that he should be a second Joseph, sold by his brothers.... Servants of God must not be judged by what their adversaries say of them, nor by the fact that one sees them succumb to calumny without any deliverance.96

In this quote Guyon distinguishes between servants of God and their adversaries. Since La Combe's enemies were some of the most powerful leaders in the French church, we can conclude that she believed many leaders of the church and of the state were not servants of God. In Guyon's implicit theology, the church contains both those who wish to serve God and those who do not. When conflicts arise in the church, she believes that the individual must trust his or her own conscience for direction. This implicit theology of a possible loss of church authority awakened fears in Bishop Bossuet. Although Guyon steadfastly asserted her faithfulness to the Roman Catholic Church, her emphasis on the primacy of the individual conscience clearly calls into question her devotion to the Roman Catholic Church episcopacy. Guyon's theology seems to contradict accepted ecclesiology through the higher value she placed on her conscience.

Guyon understood herself as a faithful daughter of the church, yet she balked and refused to assume traditional roles for women in the church. She refused submission to the traditional authority of the episcopacy and claimed the title "Spouse of Christ," although no recognized authority bestowed this title on her. Guyon lived into her theology of a new spiritual authority and a purified beginning.

Guyon's vision and theology of the church differed dramatically in yet another way from that of church leaders such as Bishop Bossuet. In her understanding of the church, both men and women could become leaders. Lay persons held as much authority as the ordained. In Guyon's mind, God's spirit dwelled inside human hearts, not exclusively in church organizations. Everyone had free access to the Word of God, whether the person was literate or illiterate. The poor and uneducated could possess special graces that the educated leaders of society did not. To Guyon true leadership came directly from the Holy Spirit.

How necessary was the Roman Catholic Church for Guyon? Throughout her *Autobiography*, Guyon asserts that her attendance at Mass was important to her, yet if a conflict occurred between a directive from Bishop Bossuet, who gave her the Eucharist, and her conscience, Guyon followed her conscience. For example, when Bishop Bossuet demanded she sign a document stating that she did not believe in the incarnation, she refused and forced the officials to lengthen the time of her incarceration. In her *Autobiography* she explains, "

> I told him I could not sign falsehoods. He answered, he would make me do it. I answered him, that I knew how to suffer by the grace of God; I knew how to die; I did not know how to sign falsehoods. He answered, that he begged me, and if I did that, he would reestablish my reputation, which they were endeavoring to tear to pieces; that he would say all the good in the world. I replied, that it was for God to take care of my reputation if he approved of it, and for me to sustain my faith at the peril of my life. Seeing he gained nothing, he withdrew.[97]

The above quote shows the strength of Guyon's convictions and belief that God works directly with individuals and not exclusively through the church hierarchy. Bishop Bossuet understood Guyon's thinking and saw the possible threat that this belief posed to the Roman Catholic Church. He mercilessly hounded Guyon about her implicit theological positions in which the church structure is not recognized as necessary for God's operations in her life.

Guyon opposed not only church leaders, but also leaders of the state. She writes of the beginning of her conflict with King Louis XIV.

> They then made known to His Majesty that I was a heretic, that I had constant correspondence with Molinos——I, who did not know there was such a person as Molinos in the world until I learned it from the Gazette; that I had written a dangerous book; and that therefore His Majesty should give a *lettre de cachet*, to place me in a convent, in order that they might interrogate me; that, as I was a danger-

ous spirit, it was necessary I should be shut up under key, cut off from all intercourse either without or within; that I held assemblies.98

A long struggle with the state ensued similar to what she had with the church. She denied that she had committed heresy and continued to protest her innocence. Guyon was subjected to aggressive interrogations during which she steadfastly and courageously denied their accusations. Guyon devalued the importance of the state in relation to her conscience, as she had done with the church.

Guyon's assertive character claims a place for her in what is now called feminist theology. She thought for herself and followed her convictions. Much of her ministry was dedicated to helping other women think and act in a similar fashion. Such was the case at the female school at St. Cyr where she helped young women learn how to pray as they learned an honorable trade to support themselves in the world.99

Guyon's feminist beliefs brought her into conflict with Bossuet. During the course of her inquisition, Bossuet told Guyon that as a woman she could not be a theologian. In her reply she alludes to the story of Balaam's ass and retorts by saying that if God could work through an ass, God could work through a woman. Bossuet wrote the mother superior Mother Picard of the Visitation of St. Mary saying that he had examined Guyon's writings "with great care; that he had not found in them anything except some terms which were not in the strictness of theology; but that a woman was not bound to be a theologian."100 Guyon quite naturally and unconsciously took on the role as theologian, even though she was a woman, and expected other persons to accept her as a theologian. Guyon felt comfortable in the role of teaching learned men such as Father La Combe and Archbishop Fénelon.

Indeed, Guyon adopted her own version of traditional, religious vows and wrote about them in her *Autobiography*. She vowed, "perfect chastity of love to God. . . . Perfect poverty, by the total privation of every thing that was mine, both outwardly and inwardly." Under obedience she promised "readily to obey whatever I should believe to be the will of God, also to obey the church, and to honour Jesus Christ in such a manner as he pleased."101 Guyon intends to obey whatever she believed was the will of God first, and then to obey the will of the church second. In actions such as these, Guyon reveals the depth of her belief that both male and female, lay and ordained, could receive the will of God.

How did Guyon arrive at these feminist, non-conforming beliefs? Her own personal sufferings opened her to acceptance of these different ideas. Also, the sight of the suffering of other women made her desire to help them through the power of prayer and acceptance of an interior life. She writes movingly of her meaningful experience of responding to the need of a physically abused launderess. This appears in Guyon's narrative as a call from God to respond to the pain of victimized women, such as abused women and child laborers. Guyon understood that these women had no legal rights to leave the abusive situations in which they lived but still struggles to help them find relief from their violent circumstances. She tells the stories of poor, working girls and women in Geneva.

> There were girls of twelve or thirteen years of age, who industriously followed their work almost all the day long, in silence, and in their employment enjoyed a communion with God, having acquired a fixed habit herein. As these girls were poor, they placed themselves two and two together, and such as could do it read to the others who could not. One saw there the innocence of the primitive Christians revived. There was in that town a poor laundress who had five children, and a husband paralytic, lame in the right arm, and yet worse distempered in mind than in body. He had little strength left for any thing else than to beat her. Yet this poor woman bore it all with the meekness and patience of an angel, while she by her labour supported him and his five children. She had a wonderful gift of prayer, and amidst her great suffering and extreme poverty, preserved the presence of God, and tranquillity of mind. There was also a shop-keeper, and one who made locks, very much affected with God. These were close friends. Sometimes the one and sometimes the other read to this laundress; and they were surprized [sic] to find that she was instructed by the Lord himself in all they read to her, and spoke divinely of it.102

Guyon's empathy for these poor and suffering women led her into a controversial, active ministry in which she advocated that women learn to place total dependence on God for their assistance both in temporal and eternal affairs. This dependence would lead to courageous changes in behavior and help them break out of abusive situations. Even as she advocated prayer, Guyon also used her financial resources to help create alternative living situations for them.

One of the last documents Guyon wrote was a short treatise on Jesus' conversation with the Samaritan woman at the well from the fourth chapter of the Gospel of John. She writes, "Christ instructs a schismatical Woman in the greatest truths, and makes her instantly an Apostle."103 Guyon labours in her theology of the Holy Spirit to open the way for all persons, including women, to be drawn to the loving Christ. She suffered excruciating agonies in this struggle and in her final days, even after protracted incarceration, she persevered in her sincere belief that even "schismatical" women could be members of the most elect Christian group, the apostles. Here Guyon's implicit feminist beliefs can readily be seen. She was not content to leave it that the woman found eternal salvation; Guyon asserts that Christ bestows still the grace of being an apostle for the Holy Spirit transcends time and place.

In summary, Guyon's implicit theology places a higher importance on her internal conscience rather than on the instruction from the church hierarchy or direction from state authorities. Her understanding of the state and its authority broke from the idea of the king being an absolute power. Guyon looked forward to a different time in history, when the vision of the church hierarchy includes both male and female leaders, a feminist perspective which brought her once again into conflict with certain bishops. This emphasis on an ensuing spiritual age and on new spiritual powers available to certain souls reveals a theology that proclaimed the advent of a different historical era, a world that would differ greatly from the one in which she lived.

Chapter Four

A University of Oxford Manuscript about Madame Guyon

Duc de Louis Saint-Simon (1675-1755), a colonel of the cavalry who was a member of King Louis XIV's court, supplies detailed information about the Great Conflict. He secretly recorded in detail the historical events as he witnessed them. Saint-Simon realized that if Louis XIV knew that he was writing a history, the king might force him out of the court. After Saint-Simon's death in 1755, his lifelong labor in these books was revealed.

The Duc de Saint-Simon vividly captured the personalities and controversies of Louis XIV's court in his *Memoirs of Louis XIV and his Court and of the Regency*. He described each individual using his particular gifts of eloquence. He described Archbishop Fénelon saying, "Fénelon was a man of quality, without fortune,——whom the consciousness of wit——of the insinuating and captivating kind——united with much ability, gracefulness of intellect, and learning, inspired with ambition." When describing Guyon he emphasized her love of solitude saying that she was "as a woman all in God, whose humility and whose love of contemplation and solitude kept her within the strictest limits, and whose fear, above all, was that she should become known." This duke understood the spiritual nature of Guyon and Fénelon's friendship, poetically describing it in this way. "There was an interchange of pleasure between their minds. Their *sublimes* amalgamated."104

Saint-Simon believed that Fénelon introduced Guyon to the court because he wanted to endear himself to Madame de Maintenon, who enjoyed the company of spiritual persons. Unfortunately, Madame de Maintenon found Archbishop Fénelon attractive, with Duc de Saint-Simon describing her feelings for Fénelon in this way. "His spirituality enchanted her: the Court soon perceived the giant strides of the fortunate Abbé, and eagerly courted him."(115) Maintenon wanted Fénelon to behave with admiration and obedience towards her. Fénelon's integrity prevented his cooperation with her ambitions.

Saint-Simon explains why Fénelon's royal favor fell dramatically after the 1697 publication of *Maxims of the Saints*. Many persons found the *Maxims of the Saints* offensive because most of the court could not comprehend what he was saying. Saint-Simon stressed that even many theologians could not follow Fénelon's intricate arguments. On the other hand, Bossuet's negative portrayals of Guyon as a nude, wet nurse in *Quakerism á-la-Mode* were easy to understand. So Duc de Saint-Simon said that Bossuet's work received a warm reception at the court, whereas Fénelon's profound theology received a rebuff from the general public. Saint-Simon wrote about Fénelon's *Maxims of the Saints* in the following quote:

> This book, written in the strangest manner, did M. Cambrai little service. If people were offended to find it supported upon no authority, they were much more so with its confused and embarrassed style, its precision so restrained and so decided, its barbarous terms which seemed as though taken from a foreign tongue,——above all, its high-flown and far-fetched thoughts, which took one's breath away, as in the too subtle air of the middle region. . . . I do not give my own judgment of things so much beyond me, but repeat what was said everywhere. Nothing else was talked about, even by the ladies; and *a propos* of this, the saying of Madame Sevigne was revived: "Make religion a little more palpable; it evaporates by dint of being over-refined.(119)

Another major issue at the Court was Madame de Maintenon's attempt to get Louis XIV to name her as queen, a request he adamantly refused. The reasons for his refusal to bestow the title of queen are varied. First, although she was a Roman Catholic, she never fully accepted common devotional practices, such as reciting the rosary and she was under suspicion of still entertaining sympathies for the Protestant religion. Secondly, as a former governess, she occupied too low of a station in society to change easily into a ruling queen. Louis XIV knew his choice of queen would be an unpopular one; his advisors did not recommend that he take this stand that would alienate many at Versailles. Finally, Madame de Maintenon's character appeared flawed to many. Nancy Mitford in her book *The Sun King* describes Madame de Maintenon this way. "She was easily influenced, a poor judge of human beings and, as will be seen, a far from loyal friend. She took people up with enthusiasm and dropped them again ruthlessly when it suited her to do so. She had an underlying melancholy, perhaps caused by the curious conflicts of her nature; and often said she wished she were dead."105 According to some scholars, Madame de Maintenon deserted King Louis XIV at the time of his death. When he lay dying, she left Versailles and moved into the school at St. Cyr.

Issues surrounding the Great Conflict still continue. In the eighteenth century after Madame Guyon's death, an anonymous French author wrote an interpretation of her life and ministry. This author attacked the accepted version of Madame de Maintenon's life written by La Beaumelle, a Danish novelist who wrote an imaginative version of King Louis' court and tried to present Madame de Maintenon as a saint. This anonymous author's insightful document adds historical information about this important era in history, as well as a probing interpretation of Guyon's life and those surrounding her.

Voltaire plays an important role in this debate over the historical workings of Louis' court at Versailles. He adamantly criticized La Beaumelle's forgeries of Madame de Maintenon's letters and led a movement against La Beaumelle's history. Voltaire was the primary advocate of publishing Duc de Saint-Simon's historical memoirs. The anonymous author adds new information and interpretation about this struggle. Later historians proved the anonymous author correct when they discovered the full extent of La Beaumelle's false handling of Madame de Maintenon's history.

This crucial document exposes details of the Great Conflict and the powerful influence this controversy over mysticism has had on history and theology.

An Eighteenth Century Manuscript

At the Oxford Bodleian Library exists a handwritten, French eighteenth century manuscript that has not been published. This manuscript is called *Supplément A la Vie Mde. Guyon suivi d' Observations sur sa Lettre a Me. De Fénelon Touchant Mme. de Maintenon*. This unusual manuscript was written in the second half of the eighteenth century and referenced in the library in 1860. The size of the manuscript is 8 inches by 5 1/4 inches. The document includes letters from Guyon to Fénelon, quotes by some persons intimately involved with this crisis, and a history of the controversy. The manuscript ends with a theological summation of what the author believed was the spiritual meaning of this long, painful controversy.106

This document includes a detailed spiritual interpretation of the controversy, providing answers about the meaning of the struggle as it was interpreted later in the eighteenth century. This manuscript was composed by an anonymous author who wrote a history of the last part of Madame Guyon's life following her release from the Bastille. This manuscript also provides additional quotations by Madame Guyon written to Archbishop Fénelon that reveal insights about her understanding of God's power and purpose in the controversy. Quotations by other persons involved in this debate shed light on the inner thoughts of persons central to this struggle.

This valuable manuscript offers significant information in several areas. First, it provides many insights into the personal motivations of Madame de Maintenon and other persons involved with this controversy. Secondly, the author composes a theological interpretation of the spiritual meaning of this painful controversy. Thirdly, the document provides additional historical information about this important controversy, balancing out the historical fantasy of La Beaumelle.

The document explains in detail how annihilation and persecution worked in this Great Conflict. Some of the questions addressed are the following ones. Does persecution stop the effectual working out of God's plan? Does persecution increase the intensity of the interior reign? What is a vocation and is it possible for a person to lose a vocation? What is the power and role of evil? How did evil operate in this controversy?

The author provides a theological interpretation of the way the events played themselves out. Because many had expected Guyon's prophecies to be realized in her lifetime, concerns existed whether this meant that Guyon was a false prophet. The author wants the readers to understand a theological interpretation that confirms Guyon's vocation as prophet.

This historical and theological document challenges La Beaumelle's writings about this controversy. In 1756 Laurent Angliviel de la Beaumelle published *Memoirs for the History of Madame de Maintenon*. The author refers to Beaumelle as a contemporary and writes of him as a "present rash writer." Because of the date of Beaumelle's document, we can speculate that this anonymous document was probably written between 1756 and 1765 about the time Voltaire was actively writing against Beaumelle's forgeries. No references exist about the French Revolution so we can assume that this is most likely a pre-Revolutionary document.

Born in Languedoc in 1726, La Beaumelle was a professor of French Literature in Copenhagen. Looking for literary projects, he visited Louis Racine, the son of the great dramatist. Racine had been collecting papers of Madame de Maintenon and gave some to La Beaumelle to peruse. In 1752 La Beaumelle published three volumes about Madame de Maintenon, two volumes of letters and one called *Memoirs for the History of Madame de Maintenon*.

Voltaire, who had himself published a history of the century of Louis XIV realized the factual problems of La Beaumelle's history. Voltaire noted the problems with Madame de Maintenon's unusual character in La Beaumelle's writing. But beyond that, Voltaire was outraged at La Beaumelle's assertion that the Prince of Bavaria was poisoned at the instigation of the Court of Vienna. Voltaire reported this to the Austrians who demanded La Beaumelle's arrest for libel from the French government. French authorities arrested La Beaumelle and imprisoned him in the Bastille. He eventually was released.

Many questioned the truthfulness of La Beaumelle's saintly portrait of Madame de Maintenon. But through an odd set of circumstances, La Beaumelle's forgeries of Madame de Maintenon's letters were discovered. La Beaumelle left his papers at the Bastille when he was released. In the 1860s a scholar, Théophile Lavallée, found these papers containing Madame de Maintenon's authentic letters and Beaumelle's forged additions to her letters done in his own handwriting. La Beaumelle stood exposed as a false historian.

This document *Supplement to the Life of Madame Guyon* attacks La Beaumelle's writings on Madame de Maintenon before they were officially discredited by the scholar Théophile Lavallée in his preface to *Correspondance Générale de Mme de Maintenon*. The anonymous author understands La Beaumelle's faulty motivation and thought, and uses this as well as other evidence to prove Guyon's innocence in this controversy. The anonymous author does not yet know that La Beaumelle created forgeries of Madame de Maintenon's letters and composed fictitious works based on these forgeries. As such, the anonymous author fills an important role in writing one of the first known attacks on La Beaumelle. La Beaumelle was later proven by history to be a fraud, as this anonymous author states.

Summary of Manuscript "A la Vie Mde. Guyon"

Nothing was ever proven against Guyon. She remained in prison more than three years after her inquisition and interrogations were finished. When she left the Bastille, she was actually in exile in her own homeland. A Scottish man André-Michel de Ramsay (1686-1743) functioned as an intermediary between Fénelon and Guyon. He also served as Guyon's secretary from 1714-1716. Chevalier de Ramsay said that she spent these years consumed with her love for God.107 Guyon continued to be "honored and respected for her good spirit, for her sincere piety, for her simple and modest virtues."(29) Ramsay said that her liaison with Fénelon continued after Guyon's release and they wrote to each other frequently. Fénelon continued to show Madame Guyon "the same friendship, the same respect, the same trust" as he had before her incarceration.(30) In their frequent letters "these mystical eagles" communicated about the experience of divine things.(41) Guyon wrote a letter of consolation to Fénelon's nephew when Archbishop Fénelon died.

Guyon's maid continued in her service until the end of her life. This maid had been separated from Guyon in prison and had experienced terrible treatment, including individual interrogations about Guyon. Guyon was continually sick after she left prison because of her poor treatment while incarcerated.

Guyon's incarceration had raised much curiosity and her books, especially *Spiritual Torrents, The Short and Easy Method of Prayer*, and *Song of Songs*, were welcomed, especially in Europe and the New World. Because of this many persons visited her in France. In particular English and Scottish Protestants came to see her, as well as going to visit Fénelon at Cambray. The author said that she visited with the English as if they were her spiritual children. Frequently the Protestants assembled in her apartment, which was illegal. They were prepared to hide in the curtains around her bed in case the authorities raided her apartment. Madame Guyon enjoyed some simple pleasures during the last years of her life. For enjoyment she gave gifts of honey that she had collected from her honey bees. She also spent much of her time with her family, friends, and neighbors.

The manuscript includes an account of Madame Guyon's final illness. She had been sick for three months. Her daughter Jeanne-Marie arrived from Paris and didn't leave until her mother's death, which was a scene filled with tenderness.

The persecution by Madame de Maintenon and the ensuing controversy drew the attention of persons throughout the world, inadvertently spreading Guyon's beliefs even further. Persons of all nationalities visited Guyon, asking her for spiritual guidance and wisdom. The author believes that Guyon's influence is powerfully seen in the Quaker movement in Philadelphia, calling it the "rule of Jesus Christ."(8)

Madame Guyon's Thoughts on the Church

The author of the manuscript considered Guyon a reformer of the Roman Catholic Church. Guyon was a prophet and a "true apostle of pure love and of divine justice" who exposed those who would destroy the true spirit of the church. Guyon spoke of a new church, not the "church as it is presented today," but of a church composed of souls acceptable to God as children.(55) The church, though, rejected her wisdom. Guyon had prophesied this, in saying that the church was falling into an increasingly corrupt state. Guyon believed that heresies had ravaged the church for false guides led the church without knowledge of God and without seeking God's will. These false shepherds destroyed the true spirit of the church and the interior reign of Jesus Christ. These prophecies about a new and pure church deeply threatened church leaders, such as Bishop Bossuet, for she offered the vision of a church that would not need their leadership. Guyon hoped for an era in which a purified hierarchy led the church. These prophecies and visions contributed to Guyon's continuing troubles with the Roman Catholic hierarchy.

Guyon, though, believed that God used even the works of these foolish leaders in establishing the interior kingdom. Madame Guyon said "that God made use of Madame de Maintenon to establish the interior kingdom, that is the one of Jesus Christ."(59) Madame de Maintenon fell away from God. From persons that fall away from God are two types: one falls into a tragedy and doesn't return, while the other strays from God and then returns.

Once the information in this document is available, the plan that Guyon and Fénelon worked towards becomes clear. They hoped that Madame de Maintenon would have remained a supporter of the interior way, gradually encouraging Louis XIV to accept these spiritual truths. Several members of the court, as we have already said, were seeking a personal piety. Because of growing numbers of persons seeking a personal holiness, and the acceptance of these beliefs by Louis XIV, a holy and righteous France would develop. Archbishop Fénelon's student (the Duke of Burgundy who was the heir to the throne) would have ruled as a servant king for his people, a theme Fénelon describes in his book *Telemachus*. But this entrancing vision of what reality could have been never developed. Instead, when Madame de Maintenon rejected the interior way of seeking God, this movement lost its power. Instead of its acceptance in France, this theology found an audience in many other places in the world. Without the persecution by Madame de Maintenon, this theology might have remained in France alone. The author compares this spreading of the interior way to Israel's rejection of Jesus Christ as the messiah. If Israel had accepted Jesus, the gospel might not have been spread to the Gentiles. Another example cited of this theology is that the persecution of the early church caused the spreading of the gospel throughout the world.

Theological Interpretation in the Manuscript

The anonymous author asserts that Madame Guyon was an innocent, sacrificial offering to God, and that her life was an immolation accepted with favor by the divine presence. In this manuscript the author raises the question of God's will in personal destinies.

The author identifies two kinds of decrees that come from God, those that are absolute and those that are conditional. An example of an absolute decree is that of Jesus' work of redemption in the world. The conditional decrees ask the cooperation of God's creatures. Those who fully cooperate with these decrees become saints. Examples of a conditional decree are the exceptional ministries the church accomplished through the obedience of extraordinary individuals. A person may always refuse to work for any conditional decrees. One example the author gives of such a refusal to cooperate is Madame de Maintenon's ultimate refusal to help spread Guyon's interior doctrine.

For the author, though, the will of God is always accomplished, even if faithless persons do not follow God's wishes. If the will of God is not received by one person or a group destined to receive the blessing of God, in another time this same grace will descend even more powerfully.

The author specifically identified certain aspects of the Great Conflict as evil. Evil was considered to be a personalized force known as Satan. The author wrote that the force of evil could not watch while God's reign was spread and attacked those who accomplished God's work. Evil stirred up the old enemies of Madame Guyon with their hope of ruining Fénelon and Guyon who had become spiritually influential in France. The author writes that Satan, knowing he has limited time, acts quickly and harshly to stop the spread of the interior realm. Satan entered individual lives, inciting their angers and passions against Guyon and Fénelon, to stop their goal of spreading the doctrine of pure love. The resurrection of Jesus Christ, though, ensures the ultimate victory of the power of God over evil. Because Satan knows his time will draw to a close, his rage is intense as he tries to destroy those who practice the interior kingdom of God. Satan uses the lives of those who allow their passions to rule them, with the goal of turning persons away from God.

The author described the personal actions of evil inside Maintenon using both psychological and theological terminology. Madame de Maintenon's God-given destiny was to work for the conversion of King Louis XIV. To follow a call requires first fidelity to God, followed by cultivation of talents received and then the acceptance of more grace. She rejected the grace necessary to accomplish her vocation. She believed that if she became queen she would be able to fulfill her role with a personal grandeur that she had desired for a long time. In about 1692 personal passions of jealousy and ambitions were awakened in Madame de Maintenon, and she started competing with Madame Guyon. Madame de Maintenon probably spoke about her personal ambitions with Fénelon who re-buffed her about these desires for personal aggrandizement. Madame de Maintenon perceived Fénelon as an ingrate who contradicted his benefactress and became his enemy. As she changed towards Guyon and Fénelon, Maintenon's heart cooled to God and she removed herself from the works of divine grace.

Guyon, though, confidently continued in her appointed ministry, begetting many spiritual children. One of these children was Abbé Gautheir. He wrote that "the one that would comprehend the annihilation of Jesus Christ in the holy sacraments comprehends also the annihilation of Madame Guyon and her godliness."(51) Guyon's books spread throughout Europe, becoming available in such places as Holland, Cologne, and Naples. Some of her correspondents included in Germany the Baron Mettervich and in France the celebrated Protestant Pierre Poiret who published her works. The author of the anonymous manuscript cites Pierre Poiret as one of Guyon's most influential followers. Poiret, a French Protestant writer who lived from 1646-1719, translated early editions of Guyon's books. Poiret believed that mysticism was the essential component of Christianity and influenced other mystics in the tradition known as German pietism.

The immolation of Madame Guyon, continues this treatise, gave off a wonderful perfume of evangelism that spread to Holland, Germany, Switzerland, and Philadelphia.108 The author believed that this divine woman helped spread the gospel through her personal immolation. The author described her contribution as a theology of innocent suffering and says that those who suffer for Christ will be surrounded by the beautiful perfume of his presence, which will draw others closer to him.

The author quotes a letter from Madame Guyon to Fénelon in which Guyon writes about the fall of Madame de Maintenon away from the grace of God. Guyon wrote, "that there are some souls that God chooses from the beginning and who are destined to a certain end, but who stray and deviate by their own fault from the way of the Lord. However, this does not prevent the truth of their vocation and grace."(66) Even if these persons leave the truth of their call behind, this does not mean that their destined goal was not achieved. For example, Madame de Maintenon was destined to help spread Guyon's theology of interior religion. Madame de Maintenon could have fulfilled this vocation by aiding Guyon, but when Maintenon did not do this, she paradoxically spread the interior doctrine through her persecution of it. He concludes that Maintenon would have accomplished more if she had not fallen, but that even with her improper motivations, God achieved his purposed objective through her. The author continued that in spite of Madame de Maintenon's intention she was an "efficacious instrument to spread the interior doctrine."(67)

The anonymous author also proposed a theology of time in this treatise. The issue for the author concerns the timing of the fulfillment of Guyon's prophecies. He states that God's timing is not foreknown, even by God's own prophets. God acts in time when he chooses, and his power descends to accomplish his purposes only when he wills. When a person rejects offered grace, the same grace descends later in time on a different person.

The author compares the delay of the fulfillment of Guyon's prophecies to the delay experienced by the apostles after the resurrection of Jesus Christ. The author makes a direct reference to this confusion over the timing of the fulfillment of the prophecies in Acts 1:6 when the apostles ask, "Lord, will you at this time restore the kingdom to Israel?" Jesus answers them, "It is not for you to know times or seasons which the Father has fixed by his own authority."

To what prophecies is the author referring? Madame Guyon prophesied that a time of greater personal holiness would occur, a time when the leadership of the church becomes less corrupt and seeks God. This would be a time when the doctrine of interior religion spreads. The group referred to as the Court Cenacle, which included Guyon, Fénelon, Maintenon, Beauvilliers, Chevreuse, and others, watched and waited for this coming time of a pure and holy leadership.

Guyon's followers thought that these prophecies would be fulfilled in their time through the leadership of the Court Cenacle and through Fénelon's tutoring of the future king of France, the Duc de Bourgogne, who unfortunately died before assuming the throne. The author, though, says that as the apostles misunderstood the timing of Jesus' kingdom, so did the followers of Guyon misunderstand when her prophecies would be fulfilled. He sees the fulfillment of her prophecies in the spreading of the interior doctrine around the world.

The author states that the approaching eternal reign of Jesus Christ is trustworthy, although the timing of its completion is not known. Those who carry God through the interior life bring the coming rule of Jesus Christ closer to consummation. In this theology of time, each era builds on the previous one to bring the rule of God closer than in the preceding era. Through the works of time, the world is building towards the fulfillment when the reign of Jesus Christ becomes visible.

The author quotes Guyon as sending a message to Fénelon that no one knows when God chooses the timing and the moments of this happening. In many ways, Guyon is reassuring Fénelon that their work had not been in vain and that their beliefs had not been inaccurate. She expresses her faithfulness that God's power continues unabated, even when betrayals and sorrows proliferate in their lives. The ministry of God working through his faithful followers cannot be stopped, because God's will always prevails.

The author describes the character and nature of persecutors. A persecutor is one who might have a vocation, a call from God, and who answers this with placing his or her life at God's disposal. At some point, though, personal passions overtake the person and he or she lives under the control of these passions. After this, the person sadly becomes a persecutor of the truth, and tries to harm those who still love God, out of the great sense of personal loss of the contemplation of God.

The document emphasizes the Platonic idea of recollection. As Plato has Socrates saying, the soul has access to interior truth. Vocations to contemplate and serve God precede birth. The author quotes Guyon saying that some souls are called at the beginning of time. The anonymous author quotes Guyon as saying that there are "souls that God chooses from the beginning and who are destined to a certain end."(59)

Yet a vocation requires the cooperation of the person with divine grace. The author describes the process of falling away from a vocation, saying that a human passion for power and control resides in the person. These passions cool and start to die under the calming influence of God. Yet throughout life, these passions may become inflamed by circumstances unless they are completely destroyed. If passions grow, they start to control the person and may destroy the interior love for God.

As Guyon and Fénelon asserted, vocations require that disinterested or pure love direct the personality. If pure love does not engage the person, baser passions rule the human being, with the lower portion of the soul ruling the higher portion. Vocations occur in the higher part of the soul, for in this portion exists the ideal of pure love. Yet even when pure love rules the higher part of the soul, the lower part of the soul still experiences the pain of sorrow and grief over human situations. A vocation from God necessarily requires sacrifices, and with these sacrifices come real feelings of grief.

The sorrow of losing a vocation turns the person into a persecutor. The mythological example of this is Satan's loss of a vocation. Sorrow at losing the eternal contemplation of God, turns into rage at those who still possess the entrancing vision of God. Guyon says that some fall away and then eventually return to God, but that some fall away never to return. Those that don't return become those that persecute godly persons.

How does the author theologically understand the concept of persecution? Persecutors still further the purposes of God, despite their intentions to the contrary. Maintenon intended to destroy Guyon and her theology, but unwittingly spread the doctrine of the interior life to many other countries. Persecutors, then, cannot obtain the destruction of godly persons but in reality help disseminate the word of God.

An example of the spreading of Guyon's theology can be seen in a popular Quaker author from the nineteenth century, Hannah Whitall Smith, in her book *The Unselfishness of God*. She wrote, "I was much helped by a saying of Madame Guyon's, that she had learned to be thankful for every snub and mortification, because she had found that they helped to advance her in her spiritual life; and in time I learned something of the same lesson."109

Who would Madame Guyon have been without the persecutions of Madame de Maintenon and Bishop Bossuet? If we speculate briefly about this, the answer becomes apparent that the persecutors of Guyon actually helped spread her theology. Before the persecution, Guyon was known in spiritual circles for her books *A Short and Easy Method of Prayer* and *Song of Songs*. She struggled with the bishop of Geneva, but had managed to keep some support from this bishop, even after her controversial stay in his diocese. Guyon was highly thought of by many other bishops and leaders of the church, and was widely invited to speak individually with persons about God.

Once the persecution started, though, Guyon sent her private *Autobiography* to Bishop Bossuet that she had written under an order from her spiritual director, asking Bossuet to keep this document in utter secrecy. Bossuet did the opposite, spreading copies of her *Autobiography* to other persons with the assumption that they would have the same critical reaction to this document as he did. Instead, others read this and recognized Guyon's spiritual gifts. Bossuet convened meetings with fellow bishops and priests, complaining of the Quietist beliefs, only to have some of these bishops support her. While Bossuet and Archbishop Harlay placed *The Short and Easy Method of Prayer* and *Song of Songs* on the Index of Prohibited Books in their diocese, other church leaders such as Bishop Camus of Grenoble admired her books.

When Madame de Maintenon continued to press for Guyon's condemnation, Bossuet utilized the ultimate weapon by holding Guyon and Fénelon's friendship up to ridicule, believing that Fénelon would save himself and desert her. Instead, Fénelon remained faithful to his friend and those who watched this controversy beheld an example of ideals lived out in the highest level of French society.

Without Maintenon and Bossuet, Guyon might have occupied a fading role in the church following Molinos' condemnation. Bishop Bossuet was himself responsible for publishing copies of Guyon's *Autobiography* and making it available to the world. He caused intense publicity that in turn motivated many to read Guyon's books. Many witnessed Guyon's calm character during her persecutions, causing them to admire her and consider her thought. Finally, Bossuet caused Rome to recognize that this obscure French widow had the full support of the respected Archbishop Fénelon. Bishop Bossuet, contrary to his intentions to stop Madame Guyon, actually helped spread her thought and the amazing story of her life throughout the world. In particular, publishers in Holland and England actively sought books about this now widely publicized controversy and were among the first to publish many of Guyon's books, along with Fénelon's writings and any document relating to this controversy.

Thus the anonymous author of this handwritten French manuscript makes a strong theological argument that through Guyon's persecutions the gospel of the interior life spread around the world, bringing many spiritual followers to Guyon. This fulfilled Guyon's visions of having many spiritual children that would survive throughout the ages.

The anonymous author offers the interpretation that Madame Guyon did not wish her disciples of other religions to convert to Roman Catholicism. Indeed, the author asserts that she asked that they remain in their own churches. This emphasizes Madame Guyon's ecumenical emphasis and acceptance of other religions. For Madame Guyon, the interior life and search for God were the crucial factors for the spiritual person. Membership in a particular church or denomination did not concern her. Her ecumenical beliefs have allowed many different groups to accept her profound theological concepts.

This author also emphasizes the joy of Madame Guyon in her final years. She spontaneously composed prayers and songs. She laughed and comforted those who stayed at her home. She raised honey bees and distributed this sweet food. The connection between annihilation and joy is similar to that of the ancient connection between sacrifice and festivals. In his work on sacrifice, the Reverend Charles P. Price emphasizes that a sacrifice leads to enhanced life. He expounds, "This central concept which has underlain the institution of sacrifice from time immemorial: the giving of life to enhance life. Sacrifice was an activity undertaken with joy, festivity and thanksgiving. New Life for Old."110 This anonymous author emphasizes that the annihilation of Madame Guyon led to a joyful life both for her and for those who followed her.

This anonymous manuscript provides factual information and an intriguing interpretation of this important controversy. *Supplément A la Vie Mde. Guyon suivi d'Observations sur sa Lettre a Mo. De Fénelon Touchant Mme. de Maintenon* now takes its place among the numerous documents produced during the Great Conflict.

Chapter Five

Madame Guyon: Spirituality for Extreme Times

As the Great Conflict raged, Archbishop Fénelon himself appealed for a ruling from Rome. King Louis XIV sent lobbyists to Rome and Pope Innocent XII assigned the matter to a committee of cardinals, who was asked to examine Fénelon's *Maxims of the Saints*. On March 12, 1699, Innocent XII issued the brief *Cum Alias*, which condemned 23 propositions drawn from Fénelon's *Maxims*. This brief was a minor condemnation of only portions of this work and never mentioned heresy, and thus was a disappointment to King Louis and Bishop Bossuet. Pope Innocent XII said about this agonizing controversy, "The Archbishop of Cambrai erred through loving God too much; the Bishop of Meaux sinned through loving his neighbour too little."111

Both Bishop Bossuet and King Louis XIV exonerated Madame Guyon during her lifetime. In 1700 when the bishops reunited at Issy, Bishop Bossuet stated that Madame Guyon had committed no wrong. King Louis XIV later released Madame Guyon from the Bastille in 1703.

How did the Great Conflict end? Bishop Bossuet never reconciled with his brilliant student, Archbishop Fénelon, and was never made the Archbishop of Paris, though that had been his goal. Bossuet struggled between recognizing the truth that with God all personal distinctions disappear at death as a river in an ocean (as he had stated in the funeral oration for Princess Henrietta) and yet seeking high positions in Louis' court and the Gallican church. He had accurately prophesied about the ultimate destruction of Versailles that he called the City of the Rich. Bishop Bossuet died in 1704.

Archbishop Fénelon remained at Cambray as a highly respected church leader. Although his banishment by Louis XIV from Versailles remained intact, Fénelon corresponded frequently with his friends from the Court Cenacle. Fénelon ministered to the many poor soldiers from the War of The Spanish Succession present in the region around Cambray. He was well-known for his ministry to soldiers from any country. Generals from opposing armies gave Archbishop Fénelon safe passage through their camps and invited him to meet the soldiers' needs in anyway he wished.

Fénelon also cared for the many poor suffering under Louis' harsh taxation plan that financed the kingdom at Versailles and his many border wars. When Fénelon encountered the homeless poor, he invited them to move into his rectory and sheltered their livestock in his courtyard. When his rectory was full, Fénelon opened up his seminary to the peasants and then purchased several homes where they could live. Many named their sons Fénelon in honor of his ministry. The Vatican's condemnation of Fénelon's theology still remains today.

According to the manuscript, Archbishop Fénelon visited Madame Guyon at least one time and corresponded with her until his death. Madame Guyon assured him that God had worked in and through their suffering, and that God alone knew the divine purposes of this historic Great Conflict.

In 1714 Archbishop Fénelon wrote a strong letter to the French Academy in which he writes about the good influence the Greek and Roman philosophers may have on issues such as rhetoric, poetry and history.112 Fénelon died in 1715, leaving little inheritance because he had distributed so much of his personal money to the poor.

Archbishop Fénelon's stand for Madame Guyon establishes him as a strong advocate for human rights. He repeatedly refused to compromise his conscience and condemn Madame Guyon in order to save his career.

Between 1709 and 1712 Louis XIV completely destroyed the Jansenist monastery at Port-Royal. He had the last twenty-two survivors dispersed, violated the tombs, took the bones to the sewer, and finally demolished the church building itself.113

Father la Combe died while still incarcerated in 1715.

King Louis XIV never crowned his wife, Madame de Maintenon, the Queen of France.

King Louis' son, the Dauphin died in 1711. Louis' grandson, the Duke of Burgundy and the former student of Fénelon, died suddenly in 1712. The heir left to Louis was his great-grandson.

At the time of his death, Louis talked to his five year old great-grandson who was his heir. Some historians report a conversation of regret from Louis.

> Mignon, said Louis VIX, you are going to be a great King. Do not copy me in my love of building or in my love of warfare; on the contrary, try to live peacefully with your neighbours. Remember your duty and your obligations to God; see that your subjects honour Him. Take good advice and follow it, try and improve the lot of your people, as I, unfortunately, have never been able to do.114

King Louis XIV died in 1715. At the time of his death, his bankrupt government was in debt by 3,000,000,000 livres. French commerce was in danger because many other European countries were at war with France and not purchasing their goods. Peasants frequently had both their cattle and land confiscated by the government because they could not pay their high taxes that financed Louis' border wars and the War of The Spanish Succession.

The costly War of The Spanish Succession finally ended with Louis' grandson on the throne of Spain. In 1718, three years after Louis' death, France went to war against Spain. Voltaire wrote about this saying "the first war of Louis XV was against his uncle whom Louis XIV had established at such cost."115 This war, known as the War of Quadruple Alliance, began after Louis' grandson, now the King of Spain, sought additional territories. Louis' great-grandson fought against his uncle and successfully stopped this expansion.

In 1762 the Jesuit order was suppressed in France, partially because of their abuse of authority when they had the ear of the King Louis XIV.116 Some historians speculate that under the Jesuits a rule had been created that allowed monarchs the right for "extra-marital monogamous relationships" because their marital duty was only to produce heirs.117 The sight of this abuse of power disturbed many at Versailles.

Madame de Maintenon died in 1719 and was buried in her school at St. Cyr. During the time of the French Revolution, angry workers opened Madame de Maintenon's grave and found her well-preserved body. They put a rope around her neck, dragged her corpse out in the courtyard and mutilated her remains. Madame de Maintenon's school at St. Cyr then became a military establishment for the education of the officers in the French army.

As we saw in the anonymous document, Madame Guyon died on June 9, 1717, in the presence of her beloved daughter, Jeanne-Marie. Jeanne Guyon and her daughter had shared many trials together, but their united suffering resulted in a lasting tenderness between them. The Great Conflict had made Madame Guyon a living legend in her latter years. Seekers traveled from all over Europe and the New World to meet with her and to talk with her about God. These religious assemblies with her were illegal and could have resulted in incarceration and death. Yet Madame Guyon continued her ministry of writing and talking about her theology. Madame Guyon lived in severe times and developed a serious theology that met the demands of her century.

Her conflict with Louis XIV is natural considering that under this king, the poor were neglected and considered of little importance. If we judge Guyon and Fénelon's theology by the fruits that came from it, their active Quietism appears quite effective. Together they built hospitals, treated Protestants gently, fed and sheltered poor peasants, and ministered to wounded soldiers. Both of them were active and effective spiritual directors to both the poor and the wealthy. They advocated for the dignity and rights of women. This is a much more expansive vision that merely ministering to the rich and privileged living at Versailles.

Historians agree that one of the greatest causes of discontent in the eighteenth century was the contrast between the lives of the nobility and clergy and those of the poor peasants. Both Madame Guyon and Archbishop Fénelon had actively spoken about these injustices to Louis. They valued changing society into a place without social barriers and divisions. They believed in justice, even while living under the absolute rule of King Louis XIV.

In this violent era, with Protestants fleeing or being massacred, with public book burnings of books on prayer, with the Inquisition threatening all who spoke of interior faith, Madame Guyon arose and spoke her words with power. Her theology tells of God who loved the poor as much as the wealthy, women as much as men, and the laity as much as the clergy. She worked as a doctor inventing medicines and as a provider making food for the starving. As she lived into this courageous ministry, her faith and her vision of a new world supported her and many others as they struggled with the dominant power of the Church Inquisition.

Both Guyon and Fénelon hoped that political changes allowing freedom would be made in their century. Louis XIV, Louis XV and Louis XVI turned a deaf ear to these pleas so instead history heard the sound of the tumbrills taking the royalty to the guillotine and the church attacked by the French Revolution.118

As Guyon said during her Inquisition, her theology was influenced by Francis de Sales and Augustine of Hippo. Augustine also writes about the spiritual crucifixion that the believer should expect using words of St. Paul. Augustine writes,

> Love makes us undergo a certain death. This death he [Paul] died who said: 'The world is crucified to me, and I to the world.' (Gal. 6:14). This death they had died to whom he said, 'You are dead, and your life is hid with Christ in God.' (Col.3:3) Love is strong as death. If therefore it is strong, it is courageous and of great power and is strength itself....Where is this love, my Brothers? In the one who does not in this life seek his own interests. (Phil 2:4, 21).119

What did her work accomplish? Madame Guyon understood God's being as the essence of justice. She writes that she experienced God's justice as a rain of golden fire. Because of this, her entire life efforts were justice for the poor, the sick, the hungry, and rights for women. Archbishop Fénelon agreed with this insight and acted with great strength in their suffering times.

Madame Guyon and Archbishop Fénelon initiated a new era of tolerance and diversity. Archbishop Fénelon advocated gentle treatment for the Protestants and no forced conversions. He recommended an educational philosophy based on recollection. Fénelon argued that girls must be educated and their needs for personal development not be ignored. In his work as royal tutor, he wrote books urging the King of France to begin dialogue with other societies and the acceptance of differences. Fénelon warned against the dangers and violence against Protestants caused by the Revocation of the Edict of Nantes. Indeed, Archbishop Fénelon argues that the "...the mere observance of outward religion is useless and harmful, if it not be animated by a spirit of love and piety within."120

Madame Guyon's skillful book *The Short and Easy Method of Prayer* tells of the possibilities of this spiritual development through recollection. The Augustinian ideal of dwelling in truth may be realized, she strongly advocates. That ideal surfaces from the human heart in a gentle spirit of tolerance. She refused to ask for conversions to Catholicism and indeed asked that her Protestant followers remain in their religious tradition and deepen whatever tradition they were in through the practice of interior religion. For example, she encouraged Chevalier de Ramsay to remain Protestant rather than converting to Catholicism.

Fénelon and Guyon both worked tirelessly to begin a new era in history when God was known within the human heart. The believer did not merely participate in a church structure but was unified now with God. Their vision was based on the Book of Revelation when the Temple disappears because the presence of God makes external worship unnecessary. Their radical vision of God realized fulfills human hopes and ends in ecstatic consummation.

Madame Guyon's theology initiated new life in a time when she feared for the future of the church. She had seen a glimpse of the possible destruction of the Christian religion under Louis XIV and consistently denounced corrupt religious leaders. Indeed, the absolutism of Louis XIV damaged the place of mysticism itself because church members feared the severe punishments meted out to those accused of Quietism. Mystical prayer went into a decline and religious rituals became dominant. Many shunned the methods of prayer that had been popular in the seventeenth century. Massimo Marcocchi writes about the effects of this controversy saying, "With Fénelon the grand era of seventeenth century French spirituality ends. . . . The condemnation by Innocent XII of twenty three propositions extracted from Fénelon's *Maximes des Saints* (1699) and the earlier condemnation of the Spaniard, Miguel de Molinos (1687), helped place these mystical movements into crisis."121

Beyond that, King Louis XIV harmed the Christian religion itself. He formed his own Gallican Church that emphasized French dominance. This church has been compared to the Nazi German Church and Japan's Shinto Religion. An aggressive nation needs a simple religion. Louis XIV's France tried to fit all forms of the Christian religion into a simple pattern that supported the state while ignoring reason and divine inspiration.

Louis also broke the spiritual authority of two popes by demanding the condemnation of the Quietists, a demand to which they acquiesced rather than lose France from the Roman Catholic Church. Louis created a culture of conformity for the French church.

Louis' support for a wealthy and privileged clergy that was removed from the intense struggles for survival of the poor also allowed the church's diminished influence. The clergy aligned with temporal power and the culture at Versailles. Also, in requiring the church hierarchy to conform to his demands, Louis created conflicts among the episcopacy. As these conflicts between arguing bishops became public, many lost respect for this church that warred within itself yet ignored the poor and starving peasants.

Louis' advisors from the Court Cenacle had seen these problems and confronted him about this; this is seen particularly in Fénelon's *Rémonstrances*. Yet Louis' response was to banish, incarcerate and kill the Quietists. What if Louis had listened to their thoughtful analysis instead? Some believe that the damages inflicted by the Sun King on Christianity continue to the present day.

Though Guyon's theology was rejected in the Roman Catholic Church, many Protestant groups received her ideas. In particular, as the anonymous author of the *Supplement to the Life of Madame Guyon* says, the Quakers in Philadelphia welcomed Guyon's theology. What made her appealing to Quakers was that she believed both in the unmediated contemplation of God, while standing up for her conscience in the face of threats from the Roman Catholic authorities. Guyon's most capable interpreter in the Quaker movement, Hannah Whitall Smith, wrote the popular books *The Christian's Secret of a Happy Life* and *The Unselfishness of God* in the late 1800s. These books are still widely circulated in the United States and Europe. Much work still remains to be done both on the depth of Madame Guyon's theology as well her widespread influence.

What did Madame Guyon help accomplish in her life and through her ministry with Archbishop Fénelon? Madame Guyon frequently dealt with several concerns and issues simultaneously. For example, she moved to the Protestant center of Geneva (an area of crucial concern to the Roman Catholic Church), teaching and writing about a method of prayer (which seemed similar to the recently condemned Quietism), traveling with a Roman Catholic priest (addressing him as a spiritual equal, even though she was a woman), and developed a ministry devoted to work among the poor (whose suffering Louis XIV infamously overlooked in his aggressive taxing program to finance his numerous wars). If one looks at Madame Guyon's life and thought, one sees the issues of her century continually acknowledged and addressed. Poverty, famine, authority of church and state, sexism, penal conditions, church struggles, and others were brought to light through Madame Guyon's books and works.

Instead of the regal dignity of church hierarchy and rituals, Madame Guyon wrote of the joys of intense communion with her friends and with God. Instead of lavish entertainments, she preferred a simple meal with her young child followed by writing books in the night. Instead of settling in a nunnery serving the church religious, she chose to be a spiritual director traveling in the world.

Guyon's goal was to communicate a different spirit to humanity than the one of her era and indeed she did. In the midst of horrific trials and incarceration in the Bastille, she remained peaceful and fruitful. Her spirit was one of happiness, as William James describes Guyon as having a "happy, native disposition" and an "admirable serenity of soul" as she goes through these strenuous trials.[122] Succeeding generations have found in her theology fresh resources for spontaneity, joy and courage in the midst of trials.

Guyon reinterpreted symbols so that religious symbols were no longer the domain of aristocrats but of the peasants. In her theology all who turned to God were chosen, including illiterates, abused children, and soldiers. Who could be an apostle? Not just a few men at the time of Jesus but any believer who stands in the presence of God. Who could be Christ? Not only one man centuries ago, but some are called to be new anointed Christs.

The anonymous document confirms this interpretation of Guyon's theology. Guyon advocated bringing the clergy among the people and not separated into a privileged hierarchy. She worked to break down the barriers between rich and poor. She did not wish for everyone to become Catholic but asked for respect for other religions. She showed a path of annihilation and pure love that leads to consummation with God and ministry to a needy world. Guyon advocated living for passionate love and the rejection of all social propriety. Find freedom, Guyon said, and be intoxicated with the presence of God.

In many ways, her words predicted the maturation of human society in what she called the coming age. She correctly identified new seeds that could change the church from within. The ideas of Archbishop Fénelon and Madame

Guyon influenced Rousseau and the early Romantic movement. Education as engaging children with the stories and the importance of feeling finds roots in the writings of both Guyon and Fénelon.

Part of the deepening of her own religious tradition was Madame Guyon's active work on the theology of evil. When evil attacks, there is no stopping the attack by reasonable solutions. Evil escalates with the attacks against her and Fénelon becoming increasingly vicious. Evil's character is that it is dynamic and intractable. Yet Madame Guyon tells us that evil is never to be feared. One potent power against evil is that of personal annihilation and acting on insights received. Evil is never to be feared, though, for the power of God is so great, that all efforts will eventually serve the purposes of God.

Madame Guyon's love for God led her into dangerous, suffering situations. Yet she writes of her sublime experience of God saying, "I loved him, and I burned with his fire because I loved him, and I loved him in such a way that I could love only him, but in loving him I had no motive save himself."123

For Guyon, God's beloved will made prison walls shine like rubies and transformed her into a divine bride from an abused teenage wife. Her God inspired beautiful, joyful songs to be sung in the fearsome Bastille. Guyon's God granted her faithful friends who reminded her of an exotic bird offering himself to her.

Guyon paid a high price for following her conscience, but she never regretted her actions and never denied the spiritual truths she advocated in her books. Guyon also continually asserted that Bossuet and others used false evidence against her in an attempt to obtain a condemnation. She wrote the following short statement about her life in her "Last Will and Testament":

> I am obliged, in justice to the Truth, and for my own justification, solemnly to protest, that false evidences have been given against me, that my enemies have added to my writings, thereby making me say things which I never said, as I was very far from thinking them. They have divers times counterfeited my hand-writing, have joined calumny to forgery, putting captious questions to me, adding to my answers what I never said, and suppressing real facts. I make no mention of the other matters. I forgive those who have been the cause of my sufferings, from the bottom of my heart, whatever they have done against me, having no will to retain so much as the remembrance therefore.124

In her *Autobiography* Guyon offered the metaphor that her soul roared with pain at the sacrifice God asked of her. This was the final answer to Bossuet for her alleged indifference to salvation. She describes her tremendous suffering, but asserted her inner certainty of eternal salvation, which was his theological objection to her theology. She describes her interior assurance of salvation.

> It is the same with the sacrifice which takes place in the trial, for then the soul is quite plunged, not only in the pain, but in the experience of her wretchedness; in a feeling of reprobation which is such that the soul roars, if one may say so: then through despair, she makes the sacrifice of an eternity, which seems to escape from her in spite of her. Nevertheless there remains to her a central depth, which says, without however consoling her: I have a Saviour who lives eternally, and the more my salvation is lost in me and for me, the more it is assured in him and through him.125

Madame Guyon believed that a new age would be coming to the church and the world that would be a new age of spiritual growth. She said that only God knew the timing of this new and spiritual age.

Their theology is not just for their era. What happened in that century show archetypal divisions that exist as religions from all eras interpret truth and the role of human effort in the search for God. The Jansenists believed in an individual piety that was fulfilled by intense, personal effort, that we might call conservative. The more liberal Jesuits practiced a moral casuistry that relieved the believer from much personal responsibility. Converse to both of these perspectives, the Quietists said to abandon one's self to God and receive the divine in contemplation. The Quietists advocate trusting in the guiding presence of God. Following the contemplation the believer moves with spiritual power into historical situations. God's pure love enters history.

These three opposing visions of human life clashed. The dissonance between them still resounds today. In the Western world Quietism only held limited influence following the Vatican's condemnation and incarceration of these thinkers.

Madame Guyon's prophecies of a more egalitarian age were certainly fulfilled. She can be understood as a post-modern thinker with a theology appropriate to today's global society. She believed in her own interior truth and recognized the corruption of the authorities of her age. She cared for her conscience above all else. She welcomed people from all religious traditions and requested that they not convert to Catholicism but remain in their own religious tradition. Church rituals held limited meaning for her and for those who followed her. These rituals were, as Guyon wrote, merely the bark on the tree.

Bishop Bossuet and others saw the implications of Madame Guyon's freethinking and attempted to stop this demanding the Vatican's condemnation of Quietism. But the Protestants, Freethinkers, early Romantics and Quietists were already too established to destroy successfully, even when the Sun King exerted his full powers. Guyon's spirit-filled theology had taken root and still influences many who search for a deeper communion with God. Madame Guyon saw what was the next mature step for Christian culture in the interior journey and took this step into spiritual power with bold confidence.

What was her vision of Christian life? Spiritual power involves seeing life through the lens of sacrifice and personal annihilation. Guyon's understanding of spiritual power advocates that if you are willing to sacrifice personally, you can make a difference in the world, and that new life springs out of the sacrifice.

Jesus understood that he could heal those who suffer if he used his energies for humanity. The Dali Lama moves in a wave of concern for Tibet and engages with the immense powers of China. Fénelon, instead of enjoying the prestige and luxury of his apartment at Versailles, sacrifices his reputation to identify himself with peasants, Protestants, and one persecuted religious woman. As Thomas Merton moves into annihilation, he begins to dialogue with Eastern religious traditions. Those who accept personal annihilation can change history and accomplish powerful goals. As Graham Greene writes in *The End of the Affair*, "The saints create themselves. . . . They are capable of the surprising act or word."126

Yet these unusual persons puzzle and intimidate some political leaders. Is this movement going to threaten my leadership, they wonder. Herod asked the wise men about the baby king and killed all male children under the age of two. Pharaoh denies Moses' request for the Israelites' freedom that leads to struggle after struggle with the annihilated Moses. The wrath of Bishop Bossuet falls upon Madame Guyon as she ministers to poor young girls at Saint Cyr and teaches them a way to personal power.

Both Madame Guyon and Archbishop Fénelon passionately advocate the force of pure or disinterested love. Fénelon describes the process of personal annihilation in his book *The Maxims of the Saints*. What is annihilation like? We have traveled to the top of a mountain, struggling up hills, making some progress with much concerted effort. This mountain is our ego. At the top of the mountain we see that there is another higher mountain peak close by. We see dazzling beauty and yearning fills our being to be in such transfiguring pure love. We feel an enveloping presence with hints of peace and joy. We turn to find our way to such a place. We descend quickly from our mountain and start falling down unseen cliffs and finding unforeseen dangers. We see hungry people and stop to feed them. We suffer injury. The journey becomes increasingly perilous. We wish to stop but at times we receive hints and traces of the alluring mountain and we continue. Yet personal suffering grows.

People everywhere are in great need! We help as we must help, and we too suffer in need.

Then finally in a burst of self-abandonment, we cry out, "My God, my God, why hast thou forsaken me?" In this trusting abandonment to God, in this honest acknowledgement of our plight, the prayer streaks like lightening to God. The divine and human unite in a powerful force for humanity. The person moves in a new spiritual sphere. The personal annihilation is complete.

Yet this journey for annihilation has no human path and no traditional way to this mountain. This ultimate journey can be compared to nothing else and the only catalyst for going is the pure love that ravishes the soul.

Political leadership that is based on the mountain of self-satisfaction and ego may decide to destroy and kill this transfigured, annihilated soul. But those living in this spiritual reality will never die, according to faithful believers. Jesus, his followers said, was resurrected. Marguerite de Porete's words still authoritatively resound advocating the annihilated life. Madame Guyon writes to Fénelon that God will use our ministry in God's own timing and way.

As the anonymous author says, some political leaders oppose those who exercise the power of personal annihilation. Yet the spiritual person may need these leaders who persecute him or her for the final stage into union with God. For in the crucible of torment and persecution, the spiritual person may truly be seen, understood and their words heard. In the crucifixion, we see the pure love of Jesus who never curses and blesses those around him to the end. In the persecution of the Dali Lama, we see patience and joy in the midst of horrific adversity. In the incarceration of Madame Guyon we still hear her singing songs of spontaneous joy as she spends year after year in the Bastille. In this archetypal experience between annihilated souls and political power, humanity glimpses traces of God revealed and involved.

The world stops in Quiet, in amazement at the sight of these virtues revealed. The words of the annihilated ones spread naturally. The anonymous author realized that in the real relationship between Madame de Maintenon and Madame Guyon, the will of God was accomplished by the spreading of Guyon's theology. This archetypal struggle exists in other relationships between political and spiritual authority. We remember also the exchange between Pilate and Jesus; the Athenian senators and Socrates; the El Salvador military junta and Archbishop Romero; the British Prime Minister Clement Atlee and Mahatma Gandhi; racist political leaders and Martin Luther King, Jr.; Chairman Mao and the Dalai Lama; the Burmese military government and Aung San Suu Kyi; and King Louis XIV and Archbishop Fénelon. In their great conflicts dwells God, the Holy One, waiting for us to turn aside and see.

The Burning Bush that preserves and never consumes, the force for humanity that carries us, calls to us out of the dance between political and spiritual power. Humanity stops in Quiet at the sight of such a conflict and sees in this dance fulfilling consummation as the divine and human unite.

The issues of the church in the era of Louis XIV are similar to the church in our time in that some of the same divisions exist. Some argue about whether spiritual growth occurs through our own efforts (as the Jansenists believed) or by understanding motivation and having minimal standards (as the Jesuits did during the time of Louis XIV). We label these groups of conservative or liberal but the ideas behind them still clash. Should we engage with high standards expecting that human beings will grow and change to meet the ideal standards, or do we destroy standards in order to make Christianity palatable?

Also, many church bishops and the hierarchy argue openly between themselves, as happened in the struggle to condemn Quietism. Hostile conflicts in the episcopacy create a climate of disdain for organized religion and may lead to a diminished place for Christianity as a whole. Historians note this happening in France so that by the end of the eighteenth century the French Revolution claimed Reason as the official religion.

Some of the human passions that engaged those at Versailles are also rampant in our culture. Many lost much money in their gambling at Versailles. The use of drugs to enhance pleasure is surely an aspect of our current culture. Is our culture lost in a furious rush for pleasure, as happened to many of those who lived at Versailles?

In our time, some also sense the power of divine Quiet. One such advocate, Thomas Merton writes of the possibilities of living directly into quiet Wisdom. In Merton's quiet contemplation he knew openness to other religions. The Taize community in 20th century France worships with simple music and the corporate experience of Quiet to which ecumenical believers flock from all over the world. The 2005 movie "Into Great Silence" received popular attention. The movie is a documentary filmed of the quiet life of Carthusian monks in the French Alps. The entire three hour movie has only two minutes of dialogue. The Washington National Cathedral opened the Center for Prayer and Pilgrimage in 1995. This quiet place is designed for worship for all religions. The now common practice of quiet Centering Prayer is now practiced throughout the world.

In many ways, our era struggles to mature into a faith that is described by Madame Guyon. Living in a forced dichotomy we splinter off into liberals who wish a greater acceptance of diversity and conservatives who wish to preserve a pure vision of the scriptures. Madame Guyon sensed similar divisions in her own time and offers her wisdom. She writes to contemplate and receive the divine wisdom. Stay in your tradition and deepen the vision without judgment of yourself or others. Embrace your annihilation and allow the movement of God within your life. Laissez faire Dieu! Do not practice the virtues but allow God to pour these virtues into your personality. Religious rituals are only the superficial bark on the tree and ought not to cause division. This God-intoxication of Madame Guyon and Archbishop Fénelon is the Great Conflict's lasting legacy.

The genius of the Sun King was that he hungered for human passion of all kinds. Was Versailles designed as a place where all human passions were released? Possibly Louis wanted to experience the deepest passions of the human heart. Indeed he set up what Anthony Levi calls a "fantasy environment."[127] In Louis' thought experiment he chose the extraordinary, the talented and the beautiful to live at Versailles. Many watched to see what would happen.

If you release the human heart from all constraints what will you have? Indeed, Louis modeled Versailles after the extravagances of Oriental kingdoms saying that he wanted Oriental splendor. Passion reigned at Versailles: passion for war, government, ballet, theater, architecture, gardens, and fashion. Also, for King Louis, the drive for enhanced sexual passion was augmented by the use of chemical aphrodisiacs.

The results of Louis' created City of the Rich were magnificent. Yet, the unexpected happened. Some say, God appeared in the midst of this unusual place. When the human heart is released, the passion for God also surfaces. Somehow this drive for God appeared amidst all of the passions and became an active power at Versailles. The faithful Court Cenacle, including many of Louis' advisors and his wife, enjoyed this passion for God known as God-intoxication. Their Quietism explored every desire and hope in the human heart.

In the time of the prophet Daniel and the court of King Belshazzar, the unattached hand appeared and wrote prophetic words on the wall. In the midst of Versailles a simple, aristocratic woman appeared and this mysterious Madame Guyon wrote words that many said were the words of God. These words ignited fiery controversies and the effects are still felt today. The unique passion of Versailles was the source for releasing the spark of Quietism into the West. These sparks landed throughout Europe and the New World.

God-intoxication is the ultimate thought experiment. Madame Guyon expressed the interior questions eloquently. What will emerge from the human heart? In light of her life, we ask ourselves: What dream are we living? On what adventure will we go?

What does Madame Guyon's theology offer each of us? In our time many seek conformity to dogma or authoritarian structures in their religious institution. Some blindly follow powerful religious leaders. With our Zeit Geist of conformity, the Quietists example minister to us. In their theology the Quietists say to find interior human passion for God and trust in this interior force to engage with history.

Madame Guyon offers the way of responsibility for one's life and full assurance that the divine wills an individual purpose for each person. These spiritual insights of Quietism lead to increased efforts for social justice, not passivity. The movements of Quietism ask each believer to give all of one's gifts passionately to the world and ask nothing in return. As Quietism finds a deep root within one's self, the person sheds a relative or selfish orientation and moves toward a light-filled higher unity.

Madame Guyon opened a window onto a different world, a world in which the traditional boundaries between cleric and lay, male or female were blurred, perhaps even erased. Guyon felt that God had annihilated her own personal will and replaced it with the divine will. This was the ultimate erasing of boundaries, the blurring of distinctions between creature and creator. Her thought and actions offered visions of a world that differed from the social reality in which she lived. In her theology the meek and lowly were ranked closer to God, and even the Sun King Louis XIV, and his wife Madame Maintenon, could not claim a privileged place before God. In Guyon's world, love between individuals is so strong that when one is in need, the other one knows it without being in the presence of the person. Through the window that she opened into another world, women can think and dream as powerfully as men. Through this open window, a person can make choices for the good of her soul while not conceding to a world threatening bodily harm. Through this opened window we see into another world where God is known and loved for who God is unconditionally, accepting the suffering that comes from this. Through this open window, God becomes one with us and is united to us following the purification of our soul. If we can accept and struggle with Guyon's theology, our religious tradition is enriched by her ideas and her challenge to seek the ideal of pure love.

In the crucible of their violent era, the words of Madame Guyon and her friend Archbishop Fénelon call humanity to pure love, annihilation of self, and prophetic acts of engagement with history.

AFTERWORD

The Rev. John M. Graham

Late in his career, Sigmund Freud came to believe that two "immortal powers," eros and thanatos, the life force and the death force, compete for hegemony in soul and society alike. In the past century the world has witnessed the destructive power of the death force in the kamikaze attacks of World War II and the suicide hijackings and bombings of more recent years.

But Freud and his followers, especially Norman Brown (*Life against Death*), understood that even though the unshackled death impulse works destruction, thanatos still holds a rightful place and can play a positive role in human affairs. Eros needs thanatos, because life without death has no meaning or lasting power. And for millennia before Freud's discoveries, of course, the way of personal annihilation——death——had beckoned those of a mystical temperament as a way to deeper union with God and God's creation——life.

Thanks to this and other pioneering works by Rev. Dr. Nancy C. James, the 17th and 18th century French writer and mystic Jeanne Guyon now assumes her rightful place among the most authoritative witnesses to the way of personal annihilation and its capacity to engender life and even the purest forms of love. James brings to her writing a special gift for connecting biography with theology. Here, she both explicates the content of Guyon's thought and movingly chronicles her suffering for what she taught and wrote. As a result, the voice of this brave and gentle daughter of aristocrats can now speak to us across the centuries more broadly and powerfully than ever before.

Some identified Guyon with the spiritual movement called Quietism, and indeed she refers to herself indirectly as a "plaything of providence" in her *Autobiography*. The Quietists taught that self-abandonment to the will of God, a quiet passivity that refuses to seek even one's own salvation, constitutes the truest union with the divine. The Roman Catholic hierarchy in the France of Guyon's time found this teaching profoundly threatening. The hierarchy's power rested on its authority to prescribe the practices and observances necessary to the seeking and attainment of salvation. Quietism presented self-abandonment as an alternative to these practices and observances. Guyon elaborated this Quietist tenet in terms of a "spiritual annihilation directed by God . . . the crucifying operations of God" in the life of the human person.

Guyon compounded her offense in the eyes of the religious authorities by publishing *A Short and Easy Method of Prayer* in 1685. The book asserted that even the unlettered can follow the mystical way of self-annihilation, through the easy method (recall the "easy yoke" that Jesus offered his followers) she articulates. The potential spiritual power of the poor and illiterate implied by this doctrine accounts for the scandal and condemnation it provoked.

We pause here to note an apparent contradiction: a "short and easy method," a set of observances and practices, to seek and achieve that self-abandonment which, according to the teaching of Guyon and the Quietists, admits of no "seeking" or "achieving" and dispenses with "observances and practices"? Here Guyon confronts the central paradox of all mystical writing and experience. The mystics have always taught us that the union with God which is the fruit of self-abandonment turns things inside-out and upside-down. In the light of this mystical union what looked like our seeking and achieving of God turns out to be God's seeking and attainment of us. The practices and observances we thought were bringing us closer to God turn out to be the crucifying operations of the divine spirit at work on us, and in us. Guyon understood, and lived, this paradox. The Austrian philosopher Ludwig Wittgenstein, reflecting more than two centuries later on language, logic and their limits in his landmark essay, the *Tractatus Logico-Philosophicus*, writes: "My propositions are elucidatory in this way: he who understands me finally recognizes them as senseless, when he has climbed out though them, on them, over them. He must so to speak throw away the ladder, after he has climbed up on it." Had Madame Guyon read these words and considered their meaning with respect to her *Short and Easy Method of Prayer* she might well have said "Amen."

Paradoxically, too, this "plaything of providence" was also a woman of action. She systematically sought out the poor and the infirm in France and beyond in order to tend to them, she raised a large family and suffered the loss of two children, she traveled widely to teach and counsel, she wrote many books and essays. Standing firmly in the mystical tradition, she shows us the dialectical unity of self-annihilation and vigorous, even feverish activity. In this respect, as in many others, her apostolate recalls that of St. Paul. "It is no longer I who live," wrote Paul, "but Christ who lives in me." Yet at the very moment when the indwelling Christ was overwhelming (crucifying) Paul's own personality, this same Paul undertook a life of unrelenting activity—traveling, teaching, writing, comforting, encouraging, suffering (in one case, he says, like a mother with her children) on behalf of the gospel.

Paul, and Madame Guyon, point us toward a fundamental truth about the Christian journey. Passivity, the soul's annihilation, its unquestioning acceptance of God's will, occurs only through active engagement with the affairs of the world. Through the world's buffetings, the "crucifying operations" of the divine spirit transform and humble the soul, turning it into an empty vessel through which the pure love of God can begin to flow.

Here again, Guyon also anticipates the teachings of a later writer whose explicit themes were philosophical but whose spirit was that of a Christian mystic. Employing a highly idiosyncratic vocabulary, the seminal American thinker Charles Sanders Peirce understood the human person per se as "firstness," or "chance"——pure ego, a world in itself. In its collision with "secondness" or "law," the ego encounters a world apart from itself, governed by ineluctable laws that the self cannot change, and is battered, reduced, annihilated. From this brutal collision the self comes to "thirdness" or "judgment," an apprehension of itself as part of a larger whole governed by laws whose purposes are still being revealed. It seems to me that Peirce's account of human growth mirrors with great precision the journey that Guyon both lived and wrote about. Guyon's initial entrancement with God's pure love, and her yearning for union with the divine lover, shows some of the naïve character of "firstness," making us think of a child living within her own world (and indeed, her cold and uncaring mother may have driven the young Jeanne to invent and dwell in such a world apart). In the crucible of "secondness," though, tested and refined by the cruel "law" of Louis XIV and Madame Maintenon's Versailles and of the Gallican church of Bishop Bossuet, Guyon's vision acquires the sort of depth and authority that lead many to heed what she says and writes. From this depth springs Guyon's gracious forgiveness of her tormenters: "thirdness" or "judgment" in Peirce's terms, the understanding that larger and mysterious purposes are working themselves our through her sufferings, and even through those who inflicted them upon her.

Madame Guyon's thought and activity also contain a powerful apocalyptic element. She looks not only to the annihilation of the individual soul, but to the annihilation of the French nation as she knew it and the birth of a righteous nation cleansed of excess and arrogance, a blessing to the peoples of the earth. Perhaps guided by her Quietist sympathies, certainly constrained by her own inherent gentleness, Guyon never sought to realize this apocalyptic vision by means other than prophetic utterance and the example of her own compassion. Perhaps, too, she foresaw the French Revolution's excesses and feared the horrific bloodshed that ensues when people stirred by apocalyptic visions seek to incarnate "the uncontrollable mystery . . . on the bestial floor" (W.B. Yeats, *The Magi*). We can take much wisdom for the living of modern life from a woman who believed with all her heart that the world was being transformed, yet maintained a modest sense of the role of human effort generally, and of her own effort in particular, in that transformation.

Finally, we consider Guyon's devotion to silence. She seems to have enjoyed the fruits of "ineffable," wordless communication with some of the souls that came under her authority. Here again, her spiritual heir Wittgenstein gives terse and bracing expression to Guyon's insight: "Whereof we cannot speak", he writes, "thereof we must remain silent. It is the mystical." And, he adds, what is mystical cannot be spoken because it must be shown. Here another key to the resolute action which sprang from Guyon's quietist passivity reveals itself. The annihilation of the soul leads us inexorably into silence. We recognize the inadequacy of our words to express that which is most true and real. We even recognize that words inevitably mislead and deceive. We understand that only action undefended and undefined by words (naked action, we could call it, because it proceeds from knowing ourselves, as Guyon did, to be naked before God) can make known the One who has called us into self-abandonment. Pierced to the heart by this realization, Wittgenstein abandoned his work of writing and teaching several times during his life to undertake menial and even dangerous work. He served as an ambulance driver on the front lines and as a hospital orderly during World War I, and as a custodian in a school run by nuns later in his life. Do we not witness here the servanthood of Guyon, among the poor village girls of Tonon, with the infirm and destitute of Geneva and elsewhere, transmitted across the centuries to a similarly mystical spirit?

The violence visited on the world by the events of September 11, 2001 and many subsequent horrific acts has revealed the destructive power of the death force, thanatos. But the yearning for annihilation need not negate life. Jeanne Guyon, by her writing and teaching, but above all by her living, reaffirmed the supreme insight of the mystical tradition across the ages: all that lives must die, but the mighty and uniquely immortal force that annihilates us also raises us up, that we might bear the fruit of purified love into a world hungry for its sweetness.

Appendix
The Oxford Manuscript Translated

Supplement to the Life of Madame Guyon,

Along with Observations on Her Letter to Monsieur Fénelon concerning Madame de Maintenon

Introduction

For a long time we have wanted to know some further details about the last years of Madame Guyon's life. We wished to have more knowledge about the persecution Madame de Maintenon (who first protected her) led against Guyon. We wanted to have details about such things as Madame Guyon's time in prison, her life in Blois, and her circumstances in that city until her death.128

Madame Guyon's charity and kindness allowed her to forgive everything, including all of the suffering others caused her. Because of her forgiveness, she did not write much about her time of suffering at the end of the third volume about her life.129 However, our debt to her memory forbids us to stay mute. We thought that others would appreciate this who, like us, respect this holy woman as the angel of the last times and who look to her as the most sure guide that interior souls can follow in order to reach God. Our oath of remembrance would only be fulfilled by gathering all that was discovered from the different details of Madame Guyon's life about which she remained silent. We have turned all our energy towards her life with the same eagerness that a present rash writer Beaumelle used in an attempt to bring back to life false and terrible lies that Guyon's enemies spread about her.130 These enemies had the audacity to besmirch Madame Guyon's character in order to defend Madame de Maintenon. This bold and self-interested writer, Beaumelle dishonestly represented Madame Guyon's writings to a community in order to maintain their founder Madame de Maintenon's glory.131 La Beaumelle used all means in his attempt to exalt Madame de Maintenon.

We will explain the causes that changed Madame de Maintenon's attitude regarding Madame Guyon, and we will also answer the slanders of this writer, La Beaumelle. Next, we will draw together all the various facts about Madame Guyon's private life at Blois. Finally, we will clarify a difficulty that Madame Guyon's enemies raised against a prophecy she made in 1689 in a letter to Monsieur Fénelon.

Supplement to the Life of Madame Guyon

Madam Guyon came forth from the Visitation convent where she had been unfairly detained because of the abominable intrigues of Father de la Motte.132 God used Madame de Maintenon and Madame de Miramion to free her.133 Madame de Maintenon was much advised to help free Madame Guyon; however, there really had to be some singular providence able to destroy Madame de Maintenon's prejudices against Madame Guyon. The whole world knew about Madame Guyon's extraordinary spiritual elevation; she reached a spiritual height that posterity would hardly believe.

Madame de Maintenon had a tremendous influence on the King's mind, which was just starting to return from his youthful distractions.134 She awakened in him some serious reflections about his company with women and on the vanity of the search for glory. This prodigal incense of glory faded leaving the King's heart changed. Everything now appeared insipid and dull to the king. Acting as a clever woman, Madame de Maintenon now excited in him sentiments of piety. People engaged him in new conversations and discourse. The court, which used to be very fashionable, started to become more religious and devoted to God.

Madame de Maintenon had her plans for the future. She felt that she no longer had youthful charms, and that the King would not fail to get disinterested finally, if she did not start to direct his attention to a different goal. She had already formed a concrete plan. Too attached to splendid and visible virtue, which in reality was a virtue like the Pharisees, too proud to be his official mistress, Madame de Maintenon was aiming at the higher goal of marrying him. She eventually obtained from him the right to marry. The marriage occurred in the year 1685, but was done in secret.135 However, no one doubted that the marriage had happened. All the court was whispering about it to each other, while pretending to ignore the marriage.

Madame de Maintenon's ambition was still not satisfied. She feared the king's infidelities and what her circumstances would be following his death. She feared that because of the inconstancy of the king, of his eventual death, and of her reputation at that time, she would only be seen and remembered as the widow of Scaron.136 Madame de Maintenon was in a delicate position. She wanted a title that would establish her position, but none other than the title of queen could satisfy her. Maybe she was wishing that this title would give her the right of Regency in case of a minority.137 However she conceived it, this was her plan, but the venture was difficult and had to be skillfully managed without rushing things. Only religious scruples could change the king's mind; therefore, she tried to turn him towards religion. She understood the fact that she had to surround him with those same religious feelings, so Madame de Maintenon finally accomplished the ascension of Monsieur de Beauvilliers, de Fénelon, de Chevreuse, de Langeron, and of several others of the first merit.138 The education of the Duc of Bourgogne also supplied a legitimate reason to place these men around the king.139

After being delivered from prison, Madame Guyon went to thank the woman who had set her free.140 Madame de Maintenon appreciated Madame Guyon's conversation. Madame de Maintenon found in Madame Guyon's conversation and exchanges something that brought her to God, and an unction that she had never felt before.

The House of Bethune (following the disgrace of the head of this house, Monsieur Fouquet, the superintendent) attended many receptions at the house of Madame Guyon's parents.141 This had created a liaison between the two families. The abbot Fénelon frequented the house of Bethune. He had the occasion to see Madame Guyon there, against whom he had many prejudices.142 These prejudices dispersed gradually and finally Fénelon totally embraced the path of the interior life.

Even La Beaumelle, in spite of all his malice, is forced to acknowledge the power that this holy woman, Madame Guyon, has on hearts. Even those who had been the most warned could not resist her words. "They saw her," he said, "listened and were disabused."143 Such avowals from La Beaumelle need to be cited. When La Beaumelle's lies and deception are exposed, they do not work to his advantage.

Monsieur de Fénelon became then the child of grace of that apostolic woman. His prejudices disappeared, and their hearts, which were only breathing through God and her love, created this divine liaison that had no other goal than eternity. We then see in the correspondence captured in the fifth volume of Madame Guyon's letters that she established with care in Fénelon's heart the supreme love of God (for whom we are exclusively made). She contributed to making Fénelon a new and better man. He did not fail to communicate to his friends the graces he had received. The Duc de Beauvilliers and the Duc de Cheuvreuses adopted these same principles.144 In helping them, Madame Guyon finished what her dear disciple Fénelon had started.

The court was taking a new shape and progress was rapid. God was known and loved, not from that love that only makes mercenaries, but from that love that forgets the self in order to give all to God. However, it was actually later in the church of Philadelphia that the reign of Jesus Christ was to make progress.145 And in the plans of God are the early promises of better times that would follow these horrible ones; in better times Satan, after having deployed all his fury, would be put to chains and God would be adored in spirit and truth.

Madame Guyon was taught these understandings of God and made her friends aware of them. She wrote about it to Fénelon. We will examine this famous letter later.

Madame de Maintenon was to be an instrument in this divine work and was working with her friends to establish in France the kingdom of Jesus Christ. The King did not oppose this, and the example of the Duc of Bourgogne, with his amended life, influenced the court and the whole kingdom.146 Indeed, Madame de Maintenon was given this same grace. Madame Guyon and her students nurtured Madame de Maintenon. As a founder of St. Cyr, Madame de Maintenon put the young students under the control of Madame de Maisonfort, a relative of Madame Guyon.147 Several of the students changed to their advantage, and nobody could turn them away from their course of action. Madame Guyon had free entrance to the school and made some really astonishing conversions. Those who read *A Short and Easy Method of Prayer* started to learn how to elevate themselves to God. All began to breathe a heavenly air. The external organization was admirable and Madame de Maintenon was proud of herself for introducing Madame Guyon to the world.

Unable to doubt the grace of that divine woman, Madame de Maintenon started to understand that what she saw of Madame Guyon's vocation to establish the kingdom of Jesus Christ came indeed from above. But the enemy of humanity was not quiet. Furious from the terrible blows its empire was getting from Madame Guyon, filled with despair from seeing the progress that the interior doctrine was making, it was only a question of finding the appropriate instruments to disturb this extraordinary work.

The ancient enemies of Madame Guyon were watching. The official La Motte and several others who had so unjustly persecuted and slandered her were terrified. They feared that their dishonesties were going to be discovered and that Madame Guyon was going to use her credits to make them known to the public, since they had used all their tricks to bring her down.

The Jansenists, who had since the dawn of ages made religion a question of party, considered all of those who did not think like them as monsters and all of those on their side as saints. The Jansenists tried in the part to attract Madame Guyon to them, but since they had failed, they denigrated her.148

Monsieur Nicole and Monsieur Boileau had seen Madame Guyon since she was liberated from the convent of La Visitation, and they conferred with her about her book *A Short and Easy Method of Prayer*.149 They were very happy with the explanations she gave them. But since she stopped doing these conferences, they cried out against her, and one published a book that was rigorously refuted by the loving Father Fénelon. They were her two fiercest persecutors. We also know that they wanted to win Fénelon. Gaining such a beautiful genius as Fénelon would have been a glorious conquest. Such a visible virtue would have given more credit to the cause of Jansenism, which had so many dreadful enemies.

Monsieur de Chevreuse had been educated at Port Royal and could not forgive Monsieur de Fénelon for not participating in this.150 For the Jansenists, it was a state crime and they were implacable. They looked with chagrin on the persons in the court who received the highest honors and favors from Madame de Maintenon, who had all power. They would wait for the most favorable moment, and if they found the occasion, try to corrupt her.

However, Madame de Maintenon seemed to have seriously embraced the path of the interior way. She saw Madame Guyon often. Their conversations awakened in her the sentiments of piety. Madame de Maintenon saw a new vision for herself, and for some time muted her ambitious views that had occupied her mind for so many years. There is no doubt that the path of renunciation and self-abandonment into the hands of God, and the fact that Madame Guyon had inculcated this in her, had suspended those ambitious views. This was the ordinary effect Guyon's grace had on hearts: to moderate, to stop the movements of nature, to pour into hearts a power and a courage exclusively made to defeat and fight spiritual enemies, which is the faithfulness God demands of all those who have been warned. But the enemy never rests, he prowls, he spies, looking for all entrances.

Madame de Maintenon was destined for important things like working for the conversion of King Louis XIV, which was no little duty. For this, she needed a peculiar grace capable to fight and to give her the appropriate efforts to sustain such a task! After the gifts are given from above, one has to show faithfulness. One has to cultivate those talents received so one can receive double from his or her efforts. Necessarily, temptation had to follow. This is the walk of grace; *for he who is not tempted, what would he know?*151

Madame de Maintenon's former views of greatness and of social elevation came back to bother her. The enemy did not miss this opportunity to play his role. He made her foresee the title of queen as a more secure foundation from which to accomplish this task of converting Louis XIV than the one God had given her. She then bonded her vocation to the greatness that she desired for so long. The net was skillfully managed and her self-love, which was still alive in her, awoke with new forces. Ambitious dreams rushed in and her passions awakened. If at that moment, the soul does not humiliate itself in front of God, in the feelings of its nothingness, she is, if not lost, at least in the most eminent danger. Spiritual pride is the most terrible enemy. Madame Guyon had written this letter about her vocation. The content was not ignored and rumors were spreading about this. Maybe still, the famous prints that her friends had engraved had added some attractiveness to her favorite project.152 In a word, the will to be declared Queen was awakening with force in Madame de Maintenon in 1692. Maybe she thought that Madame Guyon was competing in a supernatural way with her. It is more probable that she spoke to Monsieur de Fénelon to whom she tried to show the great advantages of her ambitions and the influence this would have on the Court and the entire kingdom.

Fénelon's answers were not to her taste. From then on she made her decisions by herself. She worked by the side of the King and started to put some pressure on him again. We knew her consultation with Father la Chaise, who as a perceptive and skillful man, sent the affair's decision back to Monsieur de Fénelon.153 Many writers have supported the truth of these facts which La Beaumelle rejects.154

Madame de Maintenon, who was a deceitful person and more perceptive than the King, discovered Monsieur de Fénelon's decision. It is easy to understand her indignation. She could only see him as an ungrateful person who was contradicting his benefactress. She saw in Madame Guyon a woman who forgot what she owed her. Madame de Maintenon hardened herself against them. "When one resists the Director, a cloud forms, and the grace received, leaves." At first Madame de Maintenon became insensitive, then cold, and finally walked away. But Madame de Maintenon had too many tricks to reveal herself at once. She knew how to manage the nuances of language. She did not show at first what she was really thinking because the King could have noticed the real cause.

Her desire was not to let anything be seen, to conceal her feelings and to show the opposite ones. This is so common and so ordinary at the Court that it is worthless to describe it more.

One would notice Madame de Maintenon's changes only by shades that were nearly imperceptible. She let some words escape. Since everything is picked up in the Court and everything is interpreted, those who were jealous of seeing the elevation of Monsieur de Fénelon and those who noticed that the affairs were going against their expectations, took advantage of it. Persons without principles and without morals joined this movement. None dared to attack Monsieur de Fénelon directly. He did not give any chance to others to overcome him; nevertheless, people held his success against him. People knew his attachment to Madame Guyon. People started to bring back the old traps, and soon we saw reappear those who used to persecute her but who did not dare to show themselves. However, they were ready to abandon themselves to new maneuvers and to supply spicy materials. The thing seemed easy for Madame Guyon's own brother had been the first cause of all the slander directed previously at her.155 Who would not believe a brother who was deposing against his sister that he should have rather defended? How would one not believe the theological doctors who were alarmed and talking about the changes of doctrine that were seen as new? The outburst became general. Who could exclaim the most lies?

They excited the wrath of Monsieur Godet from Marais, bishop of Chartres, who was the confessor of St. Cyr and the spiritual director of Madame de Maintenon. He was a severe man who ardently opposed all that was new. He had angrily persecuted the Jansenists. In order to make Monsieur de Chartres loose sight of the Jansenists, this shrewd and deceitful group wanted to occupy him with what they had presented to him as a new heresy.

The deceptions of the Jansenists and Jesuits caused Molinos' condemnation. Molinos had been condemned after a short period of time by the court of Rome.156 Pope Innocent XI, who was his protector, had been forced to pronounce an anathema against Molinos.157 The religious orders were alarmed. Molinos had pruned religion of all superstitious practices that were disfiguring it. He wanted to bring religion back to its true principles, such as the interior way; this is the only way to form a Christian. External practices are only the bark of the tree. People searched for crimes Molinos never committed. His extant writings show the atrocity of their slanders and the injustice of the sentence. But finally Molinos was condemned. It was because of this false crime that people accused him using their abominable and revolting judgment. When one knows a man only by the horrors his enemies pronounce, especially when the authorities are joined with them, it is easy to see why people judge superficially.

People then made the Bishop of Chartres understand Madame Guyon's doctrine as an impure one, and, to speak with the language of the time, as a true Molinism.158 People from everywhere accused her of being the leader of a terrible sect. As had already been done in the past, people sent so-called penitents to different confessors to declare themselves guilty of crimes they had done by following these principles. Several confessors of good faith had believed them, and the others who were better informed of the intrigues, were charmed by the idea of making this storm worse.

Monsieur de Chartres spoke to Madame de Maintenon with the zeal for which he was famous. Disposed as she was to accept this, she listened without a struggle, since passion colors all reason. However, it was no time to explode. Prudent and circumspect, she still wanted to watch her steps. She told Madame Guyon that the director of St. Cyr was thinking that it was wrong for Guyon to go there because it created division in the community. Madame de Maintenon said that the students did not want to listen to their teachers now. La Beaumelle added several calumnies exclaimed by Madame Guyon's enemies. According to him, the enjoyment of prayer made them miss something essential. "Instead of cleaning, one stayed lying against her broomstick; instead of taking care of the instruction of the young ladies, the others were in inspiration and were abandoning themselves to the spirit."159 However, any person who has read the writings of Madame Guyon is forced to admit by the strength of the truth, that Guyon fought against the extraordinary, including visions and revelations. There is even a whole chapter of her life that Guyon herself wrote about the subject. It was actually Madame Duperon who was making all those criminal inventions. Jealous of Madame de la Maisonfort who had won the confidence of her students, Madame Duperon was in league with the director who only wanted the rosary. Madame Duperon inflamed Monsieur de Chartres. The Bishop then reacted violently against both the students and Madame de la Maisonfort (whose confessor was Monsieur de Fénelon). Madame de la Maisonfort took back all the copies of *A Short and Easy Method of Prayer*. She did this without anger. A short time later, even Monsieur de Fénelon, who gave himself such a beautiful example of submission, asked Madame de la Maisonfort to submit humbly to these demands.

All of this violence was the work of the secret meetings of Madame Duperon, Madame de Maintenon and Monsieur de Chartres. La Beaumelle himself confesses this. Madame de Maintenon, he said, had planned it with Monsieur de Chartres. They were willing to allow Madame Guyon to write to St. Cyr, but the letters and the answers were passing through the hands of Madame de Maintenon.

However, the angry clamor about Madame Guyon was still growing outside of St. Cyr. This is what Madame de Maintenon wanted. Everyone's passions were excited so that Madame de Maintenon, who saw her work going nicely, warned Madame Guyon to retire from St. Cyr.160 La Beaumelle also adds that Madame Guyon then retired herself without regretting the loss of a world that was not made for her. Madame Guyon moved herself to solitude, ignored by men, except from Fouquet, Count de Vaux, her son-in-law; from her friend Duc of Cheuvreuse; and of her son in Jesus Christ, Monsieur de Fénelon.

Madame de Maintenon, who was encouraging this fiery controversy, had previously congratulated herself for all the good she had done for St. Cyr. But times had changed, and Madame Guyon and Monsieur Fénelon did not please her anymore. Madame de Maintenon wanted this outburst to be universal. She was enjoying her triumph in secret. Seeing them only as enemies of her views, Madame de Maintenon reasoned in the way that is natural for a soul like hers: "Monsieur de Fénelon will abandon the persecuted Madame Guyon and in that case, I will easily bring him back to me and my views. Then he will strongly hold to my views, and I will flatter him about his disgrace. I will get rid of two people that were harming my projects." When one strays from the known truth, one starts to go to extremes like this, as did Judas.

Monsieur de Fénelon was very confident since he was simple. He did not believe the warnings of Madame Guyon concerning the changes in Madame de Maintenon's attitude, maybe because he opened himself too much and because it is also difficult to remain always on one's guard.161 Madame de Maintenon did not take long to remove her mask. We see in Madame Guyon's life that when Guyon learned that her morals as well as her doctrine were being attacked, she asked Madame de Maintenon to nominate lay commissioners to examine those two subjects.

This was not in Madame Maintenon's interest. She knew very well that Madame Guyon's morals could not be criticized and that there had to be lay commissioners in order to proceed legally. Madame de Maintenon refused this legitimate request and allowed Guyon's morals to be attacked. The legal process had the right to examine both Madame Guyon's morals and doctrine. We see in Madame de Maintenon's life the reasons why she refused this demand for lay commissioners.

I will not linger on the ecclesiastic commissioners who were nominated. I will not describe the ways they proceeded. Nor will I describe the rage of Bossuet and his horrible moods whether at Paris or in the religious community of St. Marie de Meaux, where Madame Guyon had retired herself under his advice.162 Nor will I develop the causes of Bossuet's furies, or the different promises made to her, which were never kept by the Archbishop of Paris and the hats of cardinals.163 Nor will I describe all the episodes of this affair that were described by Madame Guyon with her usual charity, but who still presented Bossuet in his true colors. Nor will I present the umbrage and the jealousy Bossuet had against Fénelon. Bossuet was being eclipsed by Fénelon's writings that people wanted to read. Formerly seen as the first genius of France, Bousset started to witness in agony the disappearance of his star.

It is a horrible thing when the pride of a man aspires to be first in society and who looks at another ascending person as an enemy to be slaughtered. Since Fénelon was his rival for glory, Bossuet ceased to like him. All the personal interest in the promises Bossuet made caused his great anger. This was easy since this imperious, ambitious person never suffered from anyone's resistance, and became angry at much less than this. The fruit of all these intrigues was the imprisonment of Madame Guyon. She was incarcerated at Vincennes.164 La Beaumelle said, "It was from the solicitation of Monsieur Bossuet who surprisingly asked for a particular order that is only given with much difficulty, and that even an audacious minister would not have countersigned without fear." La Beaumelle adds that Madame Guyon was arrested and taken to the governor of Vincennes. The King, who liked the accused and hated violence, was asked by Madame de Maintenon but could not decide himself to issue such a serious order. But Bossuet alone could have overcome the repugnance of the King against this action, particularly if Madame de Maintenon inclined the King to some softness. It is true that the King wanted her sent to a convent, but did Madame de Maintenon really think the same way? This will forever make an immortal stain on the Kingdom of Louis XIV and was a horror for those who had to suffer this.

Here is what Ramsay added to this event.165 "Madame Guyon was then put into prison where she stayed for ten years. During that time they made thorough inquiries in all the places she had been since her youth. They examined all people who knew her in the provinces, whether close or far. They used threats, promises, and prisons in order to make her two maids, who had always witnessed her behavior, speak against her. Madame Guyon had to suffer fallacious interrogations by several different judges. She was transported from prison to prison to shake her confidence: from Vincennes to Vaugirard, from Vaugirard to La Bastille.166 However, the truth of her answers, the purity of her morals, the constancy of her behavior caused the bishops who reunited at Issy in 1700 to acknowledge her innocence.167 Bossuet led this meeting. However, Madame Guyon still had to stay three more years in jail after the process, where she was sick and suffering.168 The process was concluded by Monsieur de Cambray (Fénelon). Madame Guyon always begged people to tell her what her crime was and to prove that she was guilty. They finally let her out without being able to prove anything against her. She was exiled to Blois, where she spent more than twelve years being honored and respected for her good spirit, her sincere piety, and her simple and modest virtues. Even those who had the strongest prejudices against her, held her in esteem. Monsieur de Cambray (Fénelon) always had for her the same friendship, the same respect, and the same trust," said Ramsay.

Before we go on with the details that we have gathered about Madame Guyon's stay at Blois after she was liberated from prison and on the terms of her exile, we will spend some time on La Beaumelle and on the partiality of his memoirs. This deceptive writer had only the goal of writing the panegyric of his heroine, Madame de Maintenon. He disguised himself as much as possible in order to excuse his mistakes. To fulfill his goal, La Beaumelle was forced to misrepresent facts, change circumstances, frequently alter things, make ridiculous suppositions, allow himself criminal omissions, and forced to charge innocent people in order to set the guilty free. In a word, La Beaumelle was forced to abandon his holy character of historian who is only in search for truth. He delivered to us an artificially created novel that imposes on those who cannot draw on the sources, or to those who only read for their own pleasure rather than to get instructed. No doubt, he flattered himself in a rather pitiful way about his bold decisions and with his citations from other writers that he used with partiality.169 La Beaumelle could have done this to please St. Cyr that was an institution admitting only young ladies of significant families. La Beaumelle was also interested in supporting the establishment and the honor of its founder, Madame de Maintenon, and to make her into a woman of great virtue, maybe even a saint. In order to get her canonization from Rome, the question remains how to find some miracle that would prove she is a saint. The calendar would be changed by this name if a bailiff would displace a saint and put in Madame de Maintenon instead.

We will not follow La Beaumelle in all of his attacks against Madame Guyon and Fénelon since it would take us too far afield. We will choose only some of the most striking ones. We will not stop on the mocking and indecent arguments he used against the doctrine of the interior life. La Beaumelle used religious language in an ignorant and evil way, similar to the very problems he railed against. He abused mystical terms in a criminal sense which left his writings very disorderly. He wrote many mistakes and abominations. When will those who do not listen, stop judging and desecrating holy things! When will those who do not see or taste the walk of grace, stop to look at it objectively! But what really deserves the indignation of honest people is the evil false letter of Father La Combe, who, according to La Beaumelle, was reformed at Vincennes and remembered familiarities with Madame Guyon.170 First, it seems that La Beaumelle inverted the order of time. Father La Combe was not anymore at Vincennes at the time of Madame Guyon's last persecution but on a deserted island where he was exiled and seriously mistreated.171 This was during the year of 1687.172 La Beaumelle said the guarantor of this pretended letter was "the memories of the bishop d'Aven" who was suspect and known as an enemy of Monsieur de Fénelon. If this letter had really existed, its authenticity would have been recognized. Monsieur Bossuet would have known of the letter and used it against Madame Guyon. Did Bossuet need anything else to put her into jail besides this letter? Was it necessary to force her to sign false declarations?173 Without a doubt, that letter would have been produced during one of the conferences and would have caused a condemnation against Madame Guyon.

However, Madame Guyon's morals were not an issue in a declaration in 1700. Bossuet from the conference d'Issy where he was presiding sent her a declaration. "Regarding the abominations we have studied in these episodes, we have never questioned her morals. She has always shown horror at the accusations." First, had this false letter of Father La Combe's really existed, could this assembly have really suppressed it? Second, would the assembly want to suppress the letter? Third, Bossuet, who was so willing to attack her and put her in jail, would he have authorized this declaration of innocence if the letter had existed? Yet, this same Bossuet, who was the leader of the conference, sent the declaration of innocence and had given her a similar one in the past.174

Let us suppose that the letter had really existed but not the proof of its authenticity; Bossuet would have at least let the letter be publicized. Consequently, there would not have been any act of authentic innocence. La Beaumelle himself shows his perpetual contradictions when writing about what is called "Quietism." He writes, "We have seen innocence oppressed. The watchful king surprised a phantom with the heresy following relentlessly."175 And elsewhere he writes, "The morals of Monsieur de Fénelon remain clear in this quarrel where his adversaries were saying over and over that Madame Guyon's morals were lost. Those on Madame Guyon's side were avenged by the solemn testimony of the clerical assembly."

La Beaumelle wanted to exculpate Madame de Maintenon. Contradictions do not frighten him. He supposes declarations against Madame Guyon of having a licentious life. He declares things about her imprisonment. Then a little farther

La Beaumelle advances facts that destroy his odious imputation.176 Rash writer, is this how one slanders?

We cannot ignore his bold assertions that a religious from St. Cyr had given to Monsieur de Chartres a manuscript that enclosed things that made Madame de Maintenon tremble.177 If the document was indeed incriminating, why did nobody use it? This imputation shows La Beaumelle's foundation. On this handwritten memory, which has no authority, one can read what one wants. How can one tarnish the reputation of what was most clean and untouched? When will those in charge of writing history treat the truth with the respect it deserves?

I will not stop on the slanders that La Beaumelle directed against Father La Combe.178 He accused Father La Combe of being a debauchee when young. In fact, Father La Combe was seen as a saintly person everywhere he lived. The real crime Father La Combe had done was to live a life of strong regularity that contrasted with several of his colleagues. La Beaumelle also accused Madame Guyon of spending all of her days preaching. This was also the accusation of La Gauthier, of Sister Rose, and of all the troupe of forgers, who counterfeited her writings. These were the same ones who were going from confessor to confessor to attack Madame Guyon. In truth, an author that draws from such sources only deserves honest people's contempt and the public's criticism.

We can say the same about La Beaumelle's pretended justification of Madame Guyon's thoughts on royalty. In fact, La Beaumelle was forced to admit by contemporary historians that there were none. This argument was used before Madame Guyon was arrested, while she was in jail, and actually since the year 1708 during the siege of L'Ille. La Beaumelle warned the king as if King Louis XIV needed this to execute his will.

In general, La Beaumelle is destroyed by his own testimony when looking at all the sources. One source that exposes La Beaumelle's contradictions are the memoirs of Madame and Mademoiselle du Perron, who were confidantes and intimate friends of Madame de Maintenon. They were enemies of Madame Guyon and of Monsieur de Fénelon but also the enemy of the Bishop d'Aven and of the Abbot Phelippeaux.179 They said La Beaumelle was in one place a partial writer and in another place an unjust writer.

The materials of La Beaumelle's unfortunate compilation are also insulting and unfair against Madame Guyon and Monsieur de Fénelon. Let us now leave this dark conspiracy and La Beaumelle's criminal invectives. Let us finish with what we could discover about the facts of Madame Guyon's divine life from her exit from prison until her death.

We have said earlier, that after nothing could be proved against her and despite an intense criminal investigation, the bishops were forced to render their authentic testimony of Guyon's innocence. What is hard to understand is that she will stay three years more in jail after her justification because she only came out of it in 1703, even though the investigative procedure was finished with Bossuet's pronouncement at Issy in 1700.180 They finally released Madame Guyon from the Bastille and sent her on exile to her homeland. She went first to a castle that was owned by her children. From there, she was allowed to move to Blois, which was in the area. There she spent the last twelve years of her life.

We wish we had more details on those last years but she did not write anything herself. She cites that reason during those last times did not allow her to speak of this.181 She says, "I can scarcely speak, or not speak at all, of my dispositions." "All the days of those last ages of her life," cried out Ramsay, "passed in the most total consummation of her love for God. It was not only fulfilling; she was like in ecstasy. Her tables, the wainscoting of her room, everything that fell under her hand was used to write. Her happy flashes of wit and her fruitful genius filled her in a unique way." (Ramsay should have added that the Holy Spirit was guiding them). "What we have assembled from those scattered verses that escaped her out of the abundance of her heart, form today a compilation of four volumes of spiritual canticles and one other on symbols of divine love." Her state was so consumed with God that we would need to use the language of the heavens to talk about it. This is why we can only report so little. Because of this same reason our holy authors say very little on the holy Mary. We will then restrict ourselves to certain facts, which have no link between them, to satisfy the holy curiosity of the spiritual children of this divine woman.

First, it seems that her liaison with Monsieur de Fénelon continued both by written notes and by interior correspondence. Between souls of this kind, they are able to communicate whether they were close or far. They are able to feel each other and to know each other by an unknown means to those who don't have the experience. Divine activities happened between these two mystical eagles. Only eternity will make these known.

It was also said that the intimacy between Madame Guyon and Monsieur de Cambrai touched also Fénelon's nephew.182 The twenty-seven premier letters from the Fourth Volume are addressed to him, as well as the Chapters 21, 22, and 46 from the third volume. We see through those letters that the young marquis looked up to her as his mother of grace and that she had accepted that title. That correspondence lasted a long time and very likely until the death of Madame Guyon since in the year 1715 she wrote him a letter of consolation after the death of Monsieur de Cambrai.183 It seems that according to the ninth letter of this same volume, Fénelon's nephew went to visit Madame Guyon at Blois. Maybe he went there more than once. This Marquis de Fénelon had been for several years the ambassador of the General State and was killed doing valuable works in the land of Liege in 1747 during the battle of Cauffelt. Voltaire himself, the enemy of all religions, is forced to admit that, in his century of Louis the 15th, when one spoke about Madame Guyon, the young Marquis de Fénelon would start to lose his temper. He would openly say to Paris and to the assembly that Madame Guyon and his uncle were saints and that nobody had really known them.

After speaking about the Marquis de Fénelon, we will pass on to this young woman named Mademoiselle Catoz, who was recommended as a servant for Madame Guyon by Guyon's sister. Through this association, Mademoiselle Catoz was given the honor of apostolic sufferings. Mademoiselle Catoz had entered Guyon's services in 1682, as it is said in Guyon's life in the Second Tome, Chapter Nine. We also see in the Chapter Sixteen from the same volume how much Madame Guyon had to suffer for her and the resistance Catoz's propriety initially held against Guyon. Mademoiselle Catoz became one of the dear children of Madame Guyon and reached an eminent degree in her consummation in God. Mademoiselle Catoz was in prison like her mistress, and transported like Guyon from prison to prison, but separated from Madame Guyon. Mademoiselle Catoz had to suffer the most atrocious treatments. She experienced interrogations by people, who were only seeking to trap her by asking her captious questions. We see from two of Guyon's letters, which can be found at the end of the third volume of the life of Madame Guyon, the description of the state of this saintly girl. She was liberated with her mistress and followed her until Blois where she served her until she died. It seems that Mademoiselle Catoz lived a little longer than Madame Guyon did. This is all we can tell.

Let's talk now about the house of Madame Guyon at Blois. Her house was constituted with a room servant, two servants and a valet. She received some visits from the bishop, as well as from her son who had established himself not far away from this town because he had been affected by the disgrace of his mother. Madame Guyon had in her house a chapel where she did her divine services every day. This chapel being in front of her room she could always assist in them since in her continuous diseases she was able to hear them, even from her bed. She would receive the holy Sacrament from nine to ten o'clock. Who could express what was happening in that house! Nobody else than her deserved more the title of patriarch. Her house was a sanctuary where God was being served the way God should be.

The persecution of Madame Guyon and of Monsieur de Fénelon had received much attention and started many rumors. In foreign countries, some people had the curiosity to read some of her writings that had been printed, such as *The Torrents*, *A Short and Easy Method of Prayer*, and *The Canticles of the Canticles*. Their readings had made an impression on a lot of people. Several conceived the desire to see with their own eyes this woman that wrote books that had a divine unction that was not found anywhere else. People were running to her, people would write to her, and the five volumes of her letters are the truthful proof of the extent of her correspondence.

Several British and Scottish Protestants met with her during her exile at Blois. Monsieur de Cambrai and Monsieur Poiret went to visit her also. They would go to her home and they would eat at her table. Sometimes one could count seven people. One of them, Milord, stayed with her during seven years until she died.[184] He gives several particularities on his stay there. He said that among others that he paid no pension, and that the cost was so high that he could not understand how Madame Guyon, who had an annual income that did not pass over the hundred louis d'or, could handle this. He would not doubt that in fact it was a miracle that was happening then. She explains that another miracle had occurred during the life of her husband. From those gifts, she was living with those English persons like a mother with her children. We know that the English nation is not used to either discomfort or constraints, but they opened themselves to this spiritual life. Often between them they would argue and quarrel. On occasions Madame Guyon would bring them through soft words to agreement.

Madame Guyon would not forbid them any allowed amusement. When they were doing so in her presence, they would ask her opinion about these amusements. She would respond, "Yes, my children, as you wish." Then they would play their games and this great saint would stay with them while she was swallowed and lost in God. Soon those games would seem insipid to them. They would feel so attracted by the inside that they would leave everything and would stay in interior self-communion while in the presence of God who was near to her.

When one would bring the holy sacrament to her, the English persons would all be together in her room hidden behind the curtain of the bed, which had been carefully closed in order not to be seen by the priest, because of their Protestant religion. When the priest would arrive, they would lie on their knees and would be in a delightful and profound self-communion, each one according to his degree of advancement. Also, often some were in suffering that was suited to his or her state of being.

How many miracles happened during those moments that are known only by eternity? Those English persons were in a way the foundation given to the doctrine of the interior in Protestantism. It was in their favor that Madame Guyon composed several canticles appropriate to their present state. Milord Chewinkle himself said to respectable people that if someone would at that time sing to her a new "air," she would dictate a canticle on the spot, always matching the state of those to whom she was responding.

It is for them that she composed the Heroic Poem.185 Singularly the prophecy is enclosed in it.186 It is in those same views that she did the 6th speech enclosed at the head of the 5th volume from her letters, in the new edition, which was published in London under the title of *The Interior Rebutted and Researched.*

We see by those lines and by several others like them that she did not reject the Protestants and did not ask them to change their religion. She only wanted them to enter into the interior path. We know that she did not approve the change of Ramsay and that Milord Chewinkle was tempted to convert himself to Catholicism and to enter a cloister. She stopped him from doing this and predicted that he would marry. This happened eventually, since he married a rather rich woman from London. It was also said that the first child he had was brought to baptism by the woman Descheveiller, using the name of Madame Guyon, who, however dead, was envisaged as present at the baptism. This demoiselle Descheveiller was then the wife of Monsieur de Fleischlein, a very interior man, cherished and distinguished child of Madame Guyon and one of the greatest saints there was during this century.

To come back to Milord Chewinkle, he stayed at Madame Guyon's until she died, but he did not get the consolation of assisting at her last moments. He had gone to see some people that were walking in the perfection of this interior path, for according to an authentic manuscript, there were a multitude of people that had recognized Madame Guyon as their spiritual mother. Several of them were even going to Blois in order to visit her and it was there that the English persons met with them.

We know that there was a whole cloister filled with people praying and even inhabitants of the countryside who were living in the continuous presence of God. Milord Chewinkle reported that he knew a convent near Blois where all the religious were in the same interior path and that some of them were very advanced. He went there and after some conversations he told them "My dear children, what are you doing together and how do you spend your time?" To which the principal and more advanced individual of all of them answered: "Milord, we serve the good God and we crucify our selves." It was during one of those trips that the saintly mother died. Milord deeply regretted not being able to kiss her feet before she died.

Beyond those English persons about whom I have spoken, Madame Guyon had several other spiritual children. One speaks about an Abbot Gauthier from Paris that a counselor from the Count de Beslebourg named Falteman found still in 1735. Living with a certain Monsieur de Colombier, this abbot had known Madame Guyon and spoke about her in these terms: "The one that could comprehend the annihilation of Jesus Christ in the holy sacraments comprehends also the annihilation of Madame Guyon and her godliness." This Abbot Gauthier was very advanced in the interior path and much more than Monsieur de Colombier was.

Madame Guyon still had several other disciples in divers places. Monsieur the Abbot de Mateville, from Bern, returned to Blois in 1717 but found her dead. We have a few of the letters that were addressed to him in Volume 4. This abbot died in the year 1746. People say that he was a very interior person. We also count in the county of Bern a certain Monsieur Monot from Marges to whom the letter 106 from the fourth volume was addressed. Another correspondent was a lady from Venoge to whom Madame Guyon responded to a question in letter 151, volume 4. Also, she wrote to a Monsieur de Traitorrens about whom we do not know much.

She engaged in a considerable correspondence with the Baron of Metternich in Germany. We can see this in the index at the end of the fifth volume with several others.

But we should not pass under silence the famous Poiret. He composed several works on the interior doctrine, but when he discovered the ones of Madame Guyon, he felt the infinite difference that existed between his and those from that mystical eagle. He sent her works all over the world and even reprinted *A Short and Easy Method of Prayer* without Madame Guyon's knowledge in 1689. One of the friends of Madame Guyon showed her at Blois during her exile, one of the exemplars with the initial letters of his name Poiret P. P. that were generally put at the head of his books. At that moment Madame Guyon cried out, "There is the man that will publish all of my works." And indeed it was he who had done the total edition in Holland under the name of Cologne that she had never heard of before. Since then, they met. We see at the end of the fifth volume from those letters a list where it is spoken about the correspondence they had together. We know she made this a particular case. Poiret formed in Holland a patriarchal house and had an eminent piety. After Monsieur de Fénelon, he was considered as one of the most interior souls. Also, a certain Duchess de Grammont, who was looked up as a soul on fire for God, lived hidden and remote from the world. There was also a strong community in Italy in the kingdom of Naples and of Sicily. Especially after the death of Madame Guyon, those persons were unjustly persecuted under the name of Quietists. Some of them were put to death; others were sent to prison. The divine vengeance seemed to act in favor of the innocent blood. A dreadful earthquake was felt in that country at the same time making great damages in Sicily.187

Coming back to Madame Guyon, her life at Blois was simple without ostentation. Since for her all was God, or better she only saw God in everything, all reminded her of her divine spouse. But what was not seen was the level of the consummation of her state in God, in which she had made such progress that she escaped human conception and language. We can, therefore, apply what St Paul said of himself: "I do not live myself, but Jesus Christ lives in me." She was not existing anymore on the earth. Her being was found and swallowed up by God. She was the drop engulfed in a big ocean and participating in its immensity. She entered into a new life as an apostle in 1680. When we think about the facts and the number of crosses she had to bear during all that time, about the continuous sacrifices she did not cease to do in order to offer them to God, about her ten years in prison, about the nearly continuous interior suffering she endured to give birth to souls made for God and about the profoundness of her scriptures, which all announced her experiences, we can conclude, with no fear of being mistaken, that, after the holy Virgin, there has never been in this world a person of her level before. Madame Guyon was reserved in these last times to serve as an instrument of God. From her sufferings and through her divine scriptures, she served to establish the kingdom of God in hearts and to be a real apostle of pure love and of divine justice.

Let us finish what we still have to say before we stop. We know what she told in the first tome of her life, of Geneva and of the beautiful church of St. Peter that she announces will one day enclose the sublime mysteries of the Catholic religion. But no one should think that she is referring to the church as it is presented today, since, as she said in her commentary on the Book of Revelation188 18, verses 1. 2: "When will we be sure about the end of the reign? It will then be the time when the children of this church will be in a very widespread corruption." In her commentary on the Book of Revelation 12, verses 15 and 16 while talking about the heresies that have ravaged the Church Madame Guyon says that "the most dangerous are maybe the most secret." To know how Madame Guyon explains how to recognize the false doctors, the false devout that lead without knowing how, the enemies who put all their efforts to destroy the real spirit of the Church and the Kingdom of Jesus Christ and to establish their own. This prophesy does not concern the Catholic Church as it is today, but rather a real and saintly church of God composed of those who adore God in spirit and in truth. These are the only ones accepted by God as holy children. In those happy times, the exterior and the ceremonies of churches will be established in the interior, as the Holy Spirit wants it. We will then be able to say *post-tenebrus lux (after darkness, light)*.

We know that in the last years of her life she was affected by an unfortunate illness that lasted three full months. From the moment people noticed the danger, they informed the Countess de Vaux, her daughter, who came to see her. The Countess came from Paris with a very able doctor. The medical treatment Madame Guyon was given seemed to relieve her for the time the doctor was with her but the illness redoubled two days after he was gone. It became alarming with an inflammation of her throat and chest that caused her excessive pain, especially when she was given food.

A letter found at the end of the life disclosed some circumstances that we will report here. Her daughter who had come from Paris did not leave Madame Guyon until her death and expressed her deepest tenderness to her mother.189

The Countess de Vaux returned afterwards to Paris where she had become a widow after some years in her first marriage. Her second marriage was to the Duc de Sully.

Here is all that we were able to find on the circumstances of the last twelve years of Madame Guyon. They were taken from an authentic manuscript that was sent to us by one of her children of grace.

Observations on the letter to Monsieur de Fénelon concerning Madame de Maintenon

I promised to give at the end of this supplement some observations on Madame Guyon's letter to Monsieur de Fénelon and here they are.

Madame Guyon said in it that God made use of Madame de Maintenon to establish the interior kingdom, that is the one of Jesus Christ. She adds in this same letter that: "she was feeling inspired to send him this letter that there are some souls that God chooses from the beginning and who are destined to a certain end, but who stray and deviate by their own fault from the way of the Lord. However, this does not prevent the truth of their vocation and grace. Among these people there are two types: the ones that would fall in a real refusal and would never come back, and the others would only lose themselves but would come back later."

Madame Guyon added later on in the letter: "In respect of the time that these things will happen, these words have been impressed on me. We are not granted the knowledge of the time and the moment that God will reserve for His power."190

At the time this letter received much attention. The friends of Madame Guyon (who were mostly beginners) interpreted those words in such a way that they envisaged Madame de Maintenon to be the protection and the means God was going to use to establish with brilliance the kingdom of the interior in France. The historical events would reveal a very different ending.

Madame Guyon's enemies did not miss a chance to triumph over her and to accuse her of doing a false revelation. Because of their purpose we will examine this question in some detail to show the truth.

We first observe with all theologians that between the divers decrees of God, there are those that are *absolute*, others that are *conditional*. The first kind are those in which God settled the time and the circumstances. This was how his Son was sent to earth to accomplish the work of his redemption. Here everything is determined. This has to happen at a specific time and the circumstances that had to bring it were decided. However, everything seemed to happen naturally. Several other similar decrees are enclosed in our holy books.

The conditional decrees are those who ask for the participation of creatures that have been given the gift of free will. They may consequently be able to proceed or to suspend a work that in God's plan should happen differently. In conditional decrees, the persons and circumstances can vary. Therefore, these people can bring changes to the plans of God. Not that God is mistaken, since He has foreseen everything from His presence and because He has known since eternity what would happen, but God allows certain events to be disturbed because He will know in its time when to bring back the divine order.

Examples of this are in the Bible. Solomon, in the views of God, was to be an accomplished prince. He was supposed to be filled with the most exquisite graces. Solomon was supposed to be a saintly example for his subjects and an example of a true king of peace, but he lost himself and became an idolater.

Judas was supposed to be a faithful apostle but he betrayed his master.

The Jewish nation, this cherished people of God, was supposed to receive Jesus Christ, the Messiah, who was so often announced and promised in the Old Testament. They were supposed to recognize in him the character described by the prophets. The Jewish people were supposed to convert according to the prophecy of the apostles but the apostles were rejected. The apostles then addressed themselves to the Gentiles.

Here the unfaithfulness of human beings and their wickedness makes the plan for God's divine mercy to them useless. God wants the plan realized in the situation of the conditional decree, but the choice belongs to the human. However, the will of God accomplishes itself always. If persons can grasp God's decrees, they find themselves in another time. If one does not take advantage of this gift of grace and the grace is rejected, and since this grace always accomplishes its effect, that grace makes herself known in another place and time. "The fall of the Jews," says St. Paul in Romans 11, verse 12, "is the richness of the world, and their diminution, the richness of the Gentiles." And even if at the time the offered graces were not received, then another time would come when those graces would be found again and in even more abundance. This grace is like a spring that is disturbed and then releases itself with even more power.

To apply this principle to the question that we are examining, it appears that God had some plan for Madame de Maintenon to establish during that time of the Church of Philadelphia the interior kingdom of Jesus Christ. At least at the time it was supposed to happen, since before this desired kingdom should fully come, there will be a lot of events. This longed-for kingdom will only come after the strangest reversals.

Madame de Maintenon had much influence on the king's mind and, because of this, on all the court. She could be the instrument for King Louis XIV's conversion, or at least not influence him to the contrary. Perhaps with the participation of Monsieur de Fénelon, they would serve as the vehicle of King Louis XIV's salvation. This would then prove the vocation of Madame de Maintenon. At first the court progressed in the interior doctrine. Beyond Fénelon and Beauvilliers, one could see the Chevreuses, the abbots of Beaumont, of Langeron, the Dupuis de l' Echelle and several women of premier rank in the court progressing in the interior path.

The interior doctrine had also, as we have seen, deeply influenced St. Cyr. The king did not oppose this in any way. Madame de Maintenon (who was from nature an ambitious person) did shut this certain aspect of her personality for some years. But Madame de Maintenon experienced temptations, and failed because of her lack of faith. She was then rejected. This is how the walk of grace works.

Saul was destined to be the king of Israel to deliver his people from their enemies and to purge the country from the idolatry of neighboring people. He started his kingdom under the most favorable auspices, and if he would have persevered, his throne would have been strengthened. But God put Saul's obedience under trial, and he succumbed to temptation. One fall always brings along with it another fall. After Saul's fall, he is rejected. The spirit of God that had guided him abandoned him. Saul is then lost to the bad spirit, which tormented him and he became unjust, cruel and persecuted the known truth.

Had God made a mistake in choosing Saul? By no means! Saul was supposed to fulfill his vocation and he failed to do so. But the counsel of God was no less real. God's plan was not accomplished in this way, but in another way.

The prophecy of Madame Guyon was none the less certain, despite the perfidy of Madame de Maintenon. However, Madame de Maintenon was unworthy to be the instrument of this divine work. This confirms all that we have already said on the two circumstances of this remarkable letter. Madame Guyon said "that there are some souls that God chooses from the beginning and who are destined to a certain end, but who stray and deviate by their own fault from the way of the Lord. However, this does not prevent the truth of their vocation and grace. Among these people there are two types: the ones that would fall in a real refusal and would never come back, and the others who would only lose themselves but would come back later." She then added that regarding the time when these things would happen, that these words were impressed on her. "We are not granted the knowledge of the time and the moment that God will reserve for His power."

It seems evident that this prophecy was conditional and that it depended only on the faithfulness of Madame de Maintenon. However, what is trenchant in this present question is that despite Madame de Maintenon and her intention, she was an efficacious instrument to spread the interior doctrine. If she had fulfilled her vocation, perhaps she would have been hurt less. She was not worthy to be a divine instrument as seen in her duplicity. Her artifices of playing like Judas have led to similar results. Judas by betraying his divine master contributed to his own death but led to results that have been so fortunate for humanity.

In fact, here is what happened: Madame de Maintenon persecuted the interior life. She brought a lot of attention to this and excited the blind and bitter zeal from Bossuet and several others. France echoes under their clamorous controversy, and Europe watches this spectacle. Curiosity about this caused several people to procure for themselves these books that were making such a great sensation. Madame Guyon, this saintly woman, is immolated. Her apostolic suffering and sacrifices would give birth to numerous souls in Jesus Christ. The good incense of the gospel and of the interior kingdom was spreading. One sees, then, in France a number of people embracing that doctrine; from entire convents to towns, which tasted this; from people of all orders, great and small, that were getting seriously attached to it. This doctrine did not only stay centered in its own kingdom; it propagated elsewhere. The English and Scottish Protestants received this and drew close to breathe the beautiful spiritual incense. The interior doctrine appeared in Holland where all Madame Guyon's books were printed. The interior life also shaped numerous souls in Germany, in Switzerland and in several other places.

Already one could see her divers writings translated in divers languages, in German, in English, and maybe in some more other languages. We see her five volumes of letters, which has a new edition published a few years ago, and through the extent of her correspondence with many ecclesiastics, lay, Catholics and Protestants people how the church of Philadelphia had been, in secret and with no brilliance, established and received.

If Madame de Maintenon had not persecuted Madame Guyon, maybe the interior doctrine would have ended in France. This happened as well in the beginning of Christianity to the apostles who were persecuted in Judea and who brought the gospel to nearly all the known world.

This prophecy, therefore, and the kingdom of the interior accomplished itself in the middle of scorn and of persecutions, and will continue to appear in secret until the manifestation of the kingdom of Jesus Christ. That time will be marked by the wisdom and the power of God, and whoever before that time imagines himself that the propagation of the doctrine of the interior will occur with brilliance is wrong.

Humanity is naturally drawn to the marvelous and to the sensible. This prophecy needed its interpretation done by the spiritual children of Madame Guyon, most of whom were in the beginning of their path. They would only see the beauty of a literal interpretation, similar to the one of the disciples of the Saviour, who was waiting for the reestablishment of the kingdom of Israel. They liked to interpret the terms and to apply all the ideas to their time because they were only seeing a resemblance of the truth. They did not know that Satan does not let go quickly and that he was not yet put in chains. The forerunners of the visible kingdom of Jesus Christ had not yet arrived. They were not paying attention to the innumerable writings of Madame Guyon where she talks about the strange reversals and of the terrible persecutions that have to precede those happy times. They did not know that Satan enraged at seeing his kingdom ready to end would do his last efforts. But before all this happened, there would have been created several patriarchal houses where the members would lead a simple and common life in the middle of the perverse generation and of divers civil governments; the members will be adjusted without taking part in the universal corruption. Without any doubt, the light will win over the darkness until the great events that God has reserved for His power. To summarize, what was supposed to be accomplished during the time of Madame Guyon, which was the time of the church of Philadelphia, was indeed established. If this divine woman had desired that Madame de Maintenon and that the King had converted, it was in the same spirit that St. Paul wished the Jewish people would embrace the gospel and who wanted to be anathema if this would be accomplished for his brothers and sisters.—— END

Notes

1. Some major studies on Quietism are:
   Armogathe, Jean-Robert. *Le Quietisme*. Paris: PUF, 1973.
   Broekhuysen, Arthur. "The Quietist Movement and Miguel de Molinos," *Journal of Religion and Psychical Research*, 14:139-143, Jl. 1991.
   Conzemius, Viktor. *Sacramentum Mundi*, Volume 5, "Quietism". New York: Herder & Herder: 1970, pg. 169-172.
   Heppe, H. *Geschichte der quietistischen Mystik in der katholischen Kirche*. New York: Olms, 1978.
   James, William. *Varieties of Religious Experience*. New York: Collier Books. 1961.
2. Michael de Molinos, *The Spiritual Guide: which disentangles the soul, and brings it by the inward way, to the getting of perfect contemplation and the rich treasure of internal peace*, trans. by Kathleen Lyttelton (London: Methuen & Co. Ltd., 1950), 154.
3. Jeanne de la Motte Guyon, *Spiritual Letters* (Jacksonville, Florida: Christian Books Publishing House, 1982),42-43.
4. Jeanne de la Motte Guyon, *Autobiography*, vol. 1., trans. Thomas Taylor Allen. (London: K. Paul, Trench, Trubner & Co., 1898), 284-285.
5. Viktor Conzemius, "Quietism", *Sacramentum Mundi*, vol. 5 (New York: Herder & Herder, 1970), 169.
6. Marguerite Porete. *The Mirror of Simple Souls* (New York, Paulist Press, 1993), 88.
7. *Bullarium Romanum. Bull of Innocent XI Against Molinos: Damnatio Propositionum Michaelis de Molinos*, Volume 19, trans. by David Sereno, (Neapoli: H. Caparaso et Socio Editoribus, 1882), 775-776.
8. James Mudge, *Fénelon the Mystic* (Cincinnati: Jennings and Graham, 1906), 116.
9. The sources for this information about the Free Spirit heresy are Robert E. Lerner *The Heresy of the Free Spirit in the Later Middle Ages* (Los Angeles: University of California Press, 1972) and Gordon Leff *Heresy in the Later Middle Ages: The Relation of Heterodoxy to Dissent, c. 1250-c. 1450*, 2 vols, (New York: Barnes & Noble, Inc., 1967.)
10. A brief bibliography on Jansenism includes the following:
    Abercrombie, N. *The Origins of Jansenism*. Oxford: The Clarendon Press, 1936.
    Bremond, Henri. *Literary History of Religious Thought in France*. 3 Volumes, London, S.P.C.K., and New York: Macmillan, 1929-37.
    Knox, Ronald Arbuthnott. *Enthusiasm*. New York: Oxford University Press, 1950.
    Kolakowski, Leszek. *God Owes Us Nothing: a Brief Remark on Pascal's Religion and on the Spirit of Jansenism*. Chicago: University of Chicago Press, 1995.
    Pascal, Blaise. *Provincial Letters*. Edinburgh: Johnstone and Hunter, 1851.
    Sedgwick, Alexander, *Jansenism in Seventeenth-Century France: Voices from the Wilderness*. Charlottesville, Virginia: University Press of Virginia, 1977.
11. Alexander Sedgwick, *Jansenism in Seventeenth-Century France: Voices from the Wilderness* (Charlottesville, Virginia: University Press of Virginia, 1977),197.
12. François de Salignac de La Motte Fénelon, *Fénelon Letters of Love and Counsel*, translated by John McEwen (New York: Harcourt, Brace & World, 1964), 211.
13. Guyon, *Autobiography*, Vol. 2, 187.

14. Guyon, *Autobiography*, vol. 1, 9.
15. ibid., 177-180. At the request of persons who were litigating, Guyon argues twenty successful legal cases after her husband's death.
16. The *Nouvelles Catholiques* was a newly founded religious community formed from converted Protestants. Guyon lived here at the invitation of the Bishop of Geneva, Paul D'Aranthon. This community suffered from financial problems, but Guyon's powers to help this situation were limited because she had given much of her money to relatives and placed other financial resources in trust for her children.
17. Guyon, *Autobiography*, vol. 2, 41.
18. Madame Guyon never identifies this cleric by name but relates this story about protecting the nun from the attentions of this man in her *Autobiography*. This conflict with the man known as the "little Bishop" started her first troubles after becoming a widow. 282.
19. La Combe, Father. *A Short Letter of Instruction, Shewing the Surest Way to Christian Perfection*, trans. J. Gough, (Bristol: J. Gough, 1772), 301.
20. Michael de la Bedoyere, *Archbishop and the Lady* (London: Collins, 1956), 107.
21. Bossuet, Jacques Benigne. *The funeral orations pronounced at the interment of Henrietta, duchess of Orleans, and Louis of Bourbon, prince of Conde*, translated by Edward Jerningham (England: 1799), 186.
22. de la Bedoyere, *Archbishop*, 99.
23. Fénelon, *Letters of Love and Counsel*, 100.
24. Duc de Louis de Rouvroy Saint-Simon, *Memoirs of Louis XIV and of the Regency* (New York: P F Collier & Son, 1910.)
25. Fénelon, *Letters of Love and Counsel*, 211.
26. François de Salignac Motte Fénelon. *The Maxims of the Saints explained, Concerning the Interiour Life to which are added Thirty Four Articles, by the Lord Archbishop of Paris, the Bishops of Meaux, and Chartres, (that occasioned this Book,) also their Declaration upon it.* (London: H. Rhodes, 1698), 223-224.
27. Guyon, *Autobiography*, vol. 2, 314.
28. de la Bedoyere, *Archbishop*, 133.
29. Guyon, *Autobiography*, vol. 2, 321.
30. Jeanne de la Motte Guyon, *A Short and Easy Method of Prayer*, (Baltimore: B. W. Sower, 1812), 458.
31. Guyon, *Autobiography*, vol. 1, 96.
32. Guyon, *A Short and Easy Method of Prayer*, 450.
33. Jeanne Guyon, *The Book of Job*, (Beaumont, Texas: The Seedsowers, 1915), 11.
34. Madame de la Mothe Guion, *Poems*, Trans. W. Cowper, Esq. (London: Hamilton, Adams, & Co., 1837), 15.
35. Jeanne de La Motte Guyon, *The Song of Songs of Solomon, with explanations and reflections having reference to the Interior Life*, trans. James W. Metcalf (New York: A. W. Dennett, 1879), 30-31.
36. Guyon, *The Song of Songs of Solomon*, pg. 78.
37. Guyon, *The Song of Songs of Solomon*, 67-68.
38. Jeanne de la Mothe Guyon, *The Worship of God in Spirit and in Truth or, A Short and Easy Method of Prayer with two letters upon the same subject.* Francis Bailey: (Philadelphia, Francis Bailey, 1789), 166-167.
39. St. Francis de Sales, *Treatise on the Love of God*, Vol. 1, trans. John K. Ryan (Illinois: Tan Books and Publishers, Inc., 1963), 68.

40. Plato, *Collected Dialogues*, edited by Edith Hamilton and Huntington Cairns, (New Jersey: Princeton University Press, 1996), 364.
41. Augustine of Hippo, *Selected Writings*, trans. Mary T. Clark, (New York: Paulist Press, 1984), 273.
42. Guyon, *Autobiography*, Vol. 2, 62.
43. Jeanne Guyon. *A Short and Easy Method of Prayer*, 487.
44. Evelyn Underhill, *Mysticism*, (New York: New American Library, 1974), 196.
45. John Wesley, *The Works of the Rev. John Wesley in Ten Volumes*, vol. 10 (New York: J & J Harper, 1827), 320; vol. 7 pgs. 95 and 175.
46. Guyon, *Autobiography*, Vol. 2, 2.
47. Guyon, *Autobiography*, vol. 1, 69.
48. Guyon, *Autobiography*, vol. 2, 81.
49. ibid., pg. 70.
50. Guyon, *Autobiography*, Vol. 1, 65-67.
51. The main source for this is *The Affair of the Poisons* by Frances Mossiker (New York: Alfred A. Knopf, 1969).
52. Guyon, *Autobiography*, Vol. 2, 81.
53. Alphonse de Lamartine, *Life of Fénelon,* introduction to *Adventures of Telemachus*, by François Fénelon, (Boston: Houghton, Mifflin and Company, 1887), 29.
54. Guyon, *Autobiography*, vol. 2, 183-184.
55. Jeanne de la Motte Guyon. *The Mystical Sense of the Sacred Scriptures or, the Books of the Old and New Testaments (including the Apocrypha), with Explications and Reflections regarding the Interior Life,* vol. 1, Trans. by Thomas Watson Duncan. (Glasgow: John Thomson. 1872), 8.
56. Pierre Goubert, *Louis XIV and Twenty Million Frenchmen*, (New York: Pantheon, 1966), 217.
57. François Fénelon, *Selected Letters of Fénelon*, (New York: Harvill Press and Harcourt, Brace & World, 1964), 303.
58. Duc de Saint-Simon *Historical memoirs, 1691-1709*, trans. by Lucy Norton, (New York: McGraw-Hill Book Company,1967), 125.
59. Jeanne Guyon, *The Song of Songs of Solomon, with explanations and Reflections having Reference to the Interior Life*, (New York: A. W. Dennett, 1879), 67-68.
60. Jeanne de la Motte Guyon, *Autobiography*, vol. 2, 198.
61. Jeanne Guyon, *The Exemplary Life of the Pious Lady Guion*, (Bristol: J. Mill, 1806), 85.
62. Guyon, *The Song of Songs of Solomon*, 122.
63. Guyon, *Exemplary Life*, 236.
64. Jeanne Guyon, *Christ our Revelation*, (Auburn, Me.: Christian Books Publishing House, 1985), 15.
65. Madame de la Mothe Guion. "Translations from the French of Madame de la Mothe Guion" in *The Poetical Works of William Cowper*, (London: Gall & Inglis, 1881), pgs. 405, 405, 419, 405.
66. Guyon, *Exemplary Life*, 237.
67. Jeanne Guyon, *The Book of Job*, (Beaumont, Texas: The Seedsowers, 1915), 232.
68. Jeanne Guyon, *Genesis: Madame Jeanne Guyon's Commentary on the Bible*. (Auburn, ME: Christian Books Publishing House), 319.
69. Guyon, *Autobiography*, vol. 2, 328.
70. Guyon, *Poetical Works*, 27-28.
71. Guyon, *Song of Songs of Solomon*, 123.

72. Jeanne Guyon, *Christ our Revelation*, (Auburn, ME: Christian Books Publishing House, 1985), 98.
73. Guyon, *Song of Songs of Solomon*, 130-131.
74. Jeanne Guyon, *Spiritual Torrents*, trans. by A. E. Ford, (Boston: Otis Clapp, 1853), 204-205.
75. Guyon, *Christ our Revelation*, 60.
76. Guyon, *Short Method*, 458.
77. Guyon, *Autobiography*, vol. 2, 329.
78. Guyon, *Job*, 142.
79. Jeanne de la Mothe Guyon, *Spiritual Letters*, (Jacksonville, Florida: Christian Books Publishing House, 1982), 26.
80. Guyon, *Genesis*, 355.
81. Guyon, *Job*, 159.
82. Guyon, *Autobiography*, vol. 2, 174.
83. Guyon, *Job*, 165.
84. Guyon, *Autobiography*, vol. 2, 93.
85. Guyon, *Job*, 260.
86. Guyon, *Exemplary Life*, 325.
87. Guyon, *Autobiography*, vol. 2, 17.
88. Guyon says that she understood the state of some souls. For example, she knew of her father's impending death through the work of the Holy Spirit even before the news came to her through messengers.
89. Guyon, *Autobiography*, vol. 2, 82.
90. Guyon, *Genesis*, 337.
91. Guyon, *Song of Songs of Solomon*, 105.
92. Guyon, *Genesis*, 230.
93. The bishop of Geneva, Jean D'Aranthon, requested that Guyon become a nun when she lived in his diocese. When Guyon refused to become a nun, Bishop D'Aranthon, then offered to make her the mother superior of the community called *Nouvelles Catholiques*. Guyon also refused this offer. Guyon believed that God called her to remain free from religious vows. She composed and took her own vows, but refused the vows of the Roman Catholic Church.
94. Madame Guyon dreamed that she met God, whom she called the Master. She believed that the Master made her his bride and they had union with one another. She writes about this dream in her *Autobiography*, vol. 2, 54-55.
95. Guyon, *Christ our Revelation*, 23.
96. Guyon, *Autobiography*, vol. 2, 163.
97. Guyon, *Autobiography*, vol. 2, 314.
98. Guyon, *Autobiography*, vol. 2, 164-165.
99. Guyon taught her methods of prayer at the school at St. Cyr following the request of Madame Maintenon that she do so. This school was established for poor daughters from aristocratic families.
100. Guyon. *Autobiography*, vol. 2, 315.
101. Guyon, *Exemplary Life*, 234.
102. Guyon, *Exemplary Life*, 328.
103. Fénelon, François de la Salignac. *The Archbishop of Cambray's Dissertation on Pure Love with an Account of the Life and Writings of the Lady, for whose sake the Archbishop was banished from Court. And the grievous Persecutions she suffer'd in France for her religion.* (London: Andrew Bradford, 1738), 101.

104. Duc de Louis de Rouvroy Saint-Simon, *Memoirs of Louis XIV and his Court and of the Regency*, vol. 1, (New York, P F Collier & Son, 1910), 112, 115, 114.
105. Nancy Mitford. *The Sun King*. (London: Penguin, 1966), 123.
106. This manuscript was found in the Bodleian Library at the University of Oxford. The call number is MS. Add. A. 24, fols 7v-9r. The Bodleian Library has granted permission to publish this translation of the manuscript.
107. Chevalier Andrew Michael Ramsay (1686-1743) was Guyon's secretary. He also edited Fénelon's *Telemachus* and wrote *Histoire de la vie et des ouvrages de Fénelon*. Chevalier Ramsay was from Scotland. He converted to Roman Catholicism under the influence of Fénelon. Madame Guyon asked him to remain in his own religious tradition.
108. The founder of the Quakers, William Penn (1644-1718), in his 1682 Constitution in Pennsylvania upheld the basic principles of human rights.
109. Hannah Whitall Smith, *The Unselfishness of God and How I Discovered it*. (London and Edinburgh: Fleming H. Revell Company, 1903), 188.
110. Charles P. Price, "New Life for Old: Christian Sacrifice." *Virginia Seminary Journal* (December 1994): 2.
111. Bedoyere, *The Archbishop and the Lady*, 215.
112. François Fénelon, *Dialogues on Eloquence* with his *Letter to the French Academy concerning Rhetoric, Poetry, History and a Comparison between the Ancients and Moderns*, trans. William Stevenson (London: J. Moyes for W. Baynes, Paternoster-Row, 1808).
113. Pierre Goubert *Louis XIV and Twenty Million Frenchmen*, (New York: Pantheon, 1966), 275.
114. Mitford, *Sun King*, 240.
115. Maurice Ashley, *Louis XIV and the Greatness of France*, (New York: Free Press, 1946), 174.
116. ibid., 178.
117. Anthony Levi, *Louis XIV*, (New York: Carroll & Graf, 2004), 158.
118. Many historians assert that the French Revolution could have been avoided if the words of Fénelon had been acted on by Louis XIV. One source of this says "Fénelon remains the most likable personality of the closing years of the reign of Louis XIV. It has been asserted that if his constructive reform program had been realized, the French Revolution might have been prevented." *New Catholic Encyclopedia*, second edition, vol. 5, (Washington DC: Tomson Gale: 2002), 683.
119. Augustine of Hippo, *Selected Writings*, 245.
120. François Fénelon, *The Education of Girls*, trans. Kate Lupton (Boston: Ginn & Company, 1891), 77.
121. John O'Malley, *Catholicism in Early Modern History: A Guide to Research*. (Ann Arbor, Michigan: Edwards Brothers, 1988), 185.
122. William James, *The Varieties of Religious Experience*, (New York: Simon & Schuster, 1997), 231.
123. Guyon, *Autobiography*, vol. 1, 96.
124. S. Farley, *The Life of Lady Guion*, (Bristol, 1772), 267-268.
125. Guyon, *Autobiography*, vol. 2, 295-296.
126. Graham Greene, *The End of the Affair*, (New York: Penguin Books, 1951), 185.
127. Levi, *Louis XIV*, 154.
128. Madame Guyon left the Bastille on March 24, 1703. She stayed first with her eldest son near Blois. She moved to her final residence in Blois in 1705. *Ed.*

128. In 1709 Madame Guyon wrote *Récits de captivité*. This book chronicles her time incarcerated in Vincennes, Vaugirard, and the Bastille.
130. La Beaumelle (1726-1773) was a professor of French Literature in Copenhagen who wrote a life of Madame de Maintenon. Voltaire had published his *Siècle de Louis XIV* in 1740. La Beaumelle and Voltaire became enemies with their different interpretations of Madame de Maintenon. La Beaumelle was convicted of libel in another project and served six months in the Bastille in 1752. When the Bastille was stormed July 14, 1789, La Beaumelle's papers were discovered which led to the discovery of Madame de Maintenon's authentic letters and copies of La Beaumelle's fictitious letters. La Beaumelle was proven in the 19th century to have forged letters that he attributed to Madame de Maintenon. The author of this document refers to Beaumelle as young and present, so it may be concluded that this document is written before La Beaumelle's death in 1773. The document was probably written in the late 1750s. *Ed.*
131. La Beaumelle published *Lettres de Madame de Maintenon* in 1752 and *Memoires pour servir à l'histoire de Madame de Maintenon* in 1757. A short bibliography on Beaumelle is the following. *Ed.*
Beaumelle, M. de Laurent Angliviel, *Memoirs for the History of Madame de Maintenon and of the Lost Age*, 3 volumes (Dublin: A. H. Bradley, 1758).
Beaumelle, M. de Laurent Angliviel. *Lettres de Madame de Maintenon*, A Nancy: Chez Deilleau, 1752).
132. Madame Guyon was incarcerated in the Visitation convent from January 29, 1688 until September 13, 1688. *Ed.*
133. Marie Bonneau Miramion (1629-1696) distributed the alms of King Louis XIV. *Ed.*
134. Louis XIV had two official mistresses, Louise de la Vallière and Marquise de Montespan, as well as countless other affairs. Madame de Maintenon was initially the nanny for his children by Montespan. *Ed.*
135. King Louis XIV married Madame de Maintenon who was a governess in his court secretly in the presence of only a few witnesses, one of whom probably was Archbishop Harlay of Paris. All records of the marriage were destroyed. The morganatic marriage was never publicized in France, since Louis realized the marriage would not be popular in the royal court because Maintenon's previous position had been a low one. Madame de Maintenon's thwarted desire to be named queen of France played a significant role in this controversy. *Ed.*
136. Madame de Maintenon had been married to Paul Scarron from April 4, 1652 until his death on October 6, 1660. This anonymous author spells the name Scaron. *Ed.*
137. Philippe, Duc d'Orleans became Regent after the death of Louis XIV on September 1, 1715. Madame de Maintenon had to negotiate her finances and her position with the Duc d'Orleans. She neither respected nor liked the Duc d'Orleans. *Ed.*
138. Madame de Maintenon was displeased with these men when they refused to support her in her attacks on Fénelon. She attempted to bring about the disgrace of Beauvilliers but the King trusted and respected Beauvilliers too much to allow his personal ruin. King Louis XIV did dismiss many of Fénelon's friends and relatives including de Langeron who was considered to be Fénelon's closest friend. Louis also dismissed Fénelon's nephew and brother. A plea was made to continue their salaries but Louis rejected this request. *Ed.*
139. King Louis XIV made Fénelon tutor to his grandson, the Duc de Bourgogne and his brothers, on August 16, 1689, at the request of Madame de Maintenon. *Ed.*

140. Madame Guyon was released from her incarceration in the Visitation Convent in 1688. *Ed.*
141. Nicolas Fouquet (1615-1680) was removed from his position as King Louis XIV's Minister of Finance and jailed. He was imprisoned in 1665 and remained there until his death. Fouquet's daughter, the Duchess of Bethune, was still received at court. She had found refuge in Montargis with Guyon's parents. *Ed.*
142. Fénelon met Madame Guyon early in October, 1688, at the home of Duchesse de Béthune-Charost at Beynes near Versailles. The Duchess was the daughter of Fouquet. *Ed.*
143. In the original document the footnote reads, "See *Memoirs of Madame de Maintenon*, Tome 4, Chapter 4."
144. Paul, Comte de Saint-Aignan, Duc de Beauvilliers, was known as the Good Duke. He spoke openly to the King and was known for siding with the poor. Louis made him a Minister of State in 1692. Along with his wife, Beauvilliers was a good friend of Madame de Maintenon. Charles, Honoré d'Albert, Duc de Chevreuse and his wife were also close friends with Madame de Maintenon, along with the Beauvilliers. Both the Duc de Chevreuse and the Duc de Beauvilliers committed themselves to high ethical standards while remaining in the king's service and surrounded themselves with similar high-minded individuals, believing that this purified hierarchy was called to rule France in a new age. Many called this group the Court Cenacle. *Ed.*
145. Prominent Quaker authors such as Hannah Whitall Smith acknowledge the influence of Fénelon and Guyon. *Ed.*
146. Both the historian Saint-Simon and Madame de Maintenon write of the dramatic, good change in the Duc de Bourgogne's character and behavior after Fénelon became the duke's tutor. *Ed.*
147. Madame de La Maisonfort was a cousin of Madame Guyon. Madame de La Mainsonfort was a popular teacher at St. Cyr who worked tirelessly for the release of Madame Guyon. *Ed.*
148. In the original document the footnote reads, "Life, 1st Tome, Chapter 24, V. 4."
149. Madame Guyon met with the Jansenist theologians Pierre Nicole and Nicolas Boileau in the summer of 1693. The author assumes that the reader knows that Nicole and Boileau are Jansenists. Pierre Nicole was a famous moralist. Nicholas Boileau (called Boileau-Despréaux) was a satiric poet who was appointed to be one of the King's historiographers along with his close friend, Jean Racine. Boileau corrected the language of the constitution at Madame de Maintenon's school at St. Cyr. Nicole and Boileau advised Guyon that the only thing wrong with her book *A Short and Easy Method of Prayer* was that their was a lack of sufficient explanation of the terms and the teaching. Following that, Madame Guyon wrote *A Short Defense of A Short and Easy Method of Prayer. Ed.*
150. According to Saint-Simon, the Duc de Chevreuse practiced his religious beliefs intelligently. This document is historically accurate that the Duc de Chevreuse was educated at the Jansenist school in Port Royal.
151. In the original document this statement is underlined. *Ed.*
152. In the original document the footnote reads, "Cantiques de Madame Guyon, Tome Peu. Frontispiece."
153. Father François de La Chaise was Louis XIV's Jesuit confessor. *Ed.*
154. In the original document the footnote reads, "Memoire, Book 10, Chapter 12, La Beaumelle after having reported the fact rejects it as impossible."

155. Madame Guyon's half-brother, the Père de La Motte, was a member of the Barnabite Order in Paris. He actively sought her arrest and caused many of her problems. *Ed.*
156. Molinos was arrested on July 16, 1685. Michael de Molinos' major work is *The Spiritual Guide which disentangles the soul and brings it by the inward way to the getting of perfect contemplation and the rich treasure of internal peace.* London: Methune & Co. Ltd., 1950. In this sentence the author wrote the term "Jacobites" rather than Jansenists. This appears to be a mistake in the handwritten document. The anonymous author clearly means Jansenists since that is the point he is trying to make in this section of the document. Also, the Jacobites did not appear until after the revolution of 1688; Molinos' condemnation happened in 1687. *Ed.*
157. Molinos' condemnation happened in 1687 in "Coelestis Pastor" written by Innocent XI. *Ed.*
158. Paul des Marais Godet was the Bishop of Chartres from 1690. He was also the confessor of Madame de Maintenon. *Ed.*
159. In the original document the footnote reads, "Memoire de Maintenon, Book 4, Chapter 7."
160. Madame de Maintenon sent an order to Madame Guyon on May 2, 1693, telling her never to return to St. Cyr. Madame Guyon complied with this order. *Ed.*
161. In the original document the footnote reads, "Life, Book 3, Chapter 16."
162. Madame Guyon arrived at Meaux on January 13, 1695. *Ed.*
163. Harlay de Champvallon (1625-1695) was the Archbishop of Paris. He arrested Father la Combe in 1687. He also condemned Madame Guyon's writings. During Madame Guyon's first incarceration Archbishop Harlay offered her freedom if she consented to the marriage of her heiress daughter to the Archbishop's nephew. Madame Guyon adamantly refused this offer, saying that she would prefer to remain incarcerated than allow this marriage. Archbishop Harlay played a large part in this controversy. *Ed.*
164. Madame Guyon was incarcerated in the Vincennes on December 31, 1695, and interrogated by the chief of police La Reynie. *Ed.*
165. In the original document the footnote reads, "Ramsay, Life of Fénelon, page 100."
166. Madame Guyon was moved from Vincennes to Vaugirard on October 16, 1696. On June 4, 1698, she was taken to the Bastille. *Ed.*
167. The original Issy conferences included Bossuet; de Noailles, the bishop of Châlons; Tronson, the superior of Saint-Sulpice and a former professor of Fénelon; and Archbishop Fénelon. These original conferences ran from July, 1694, until March, 1695. At the Assembly of Bishops in 1700, Bossuet acknowledged Fénelon's submission and Guyon's innocence. Bossuet's quote given in this document about Guyon is historically accurate. *Ed.*
168. Guyon was detained three more years after Bossuet's admission because King Louis XIV and Madame de Maintenon did not want her released from the Bastille. Madame Guyon was finally released from the Bastille on March 24, 1703. She was removed from the prison lying sick on a litter. *Ed.*
169. In the original document the footnote reads, "See what he says of de Phelippeaux his guarantor of facts before God, Book 10, Chapters 1 and 4."
170. On May 14, 1698, Madame Guyon was presented with a letter said to be written by Father La Combe. She said it was false. During Bishop Bossuet's campaign at the Vatican to have Fénelon's book *The Maxims of the Saints* condemned, the nephew

of Bishop Bossuet presented a copy of this letter to Pope Innocent XII as evidence against Madame Guyon and Archbishop Fénelon. *Ed.*
171. Father La Combe was initially arrested on October 3, 1687. On April 26, 1698, he was removed from the prison at Lourdes and taken to the Vincennes. Father La Combe died on June 29, 1715. *Ed.*
172. In the original document the footnote reads, "This last persecution falls in 1695."
173. In the original document the footnote reads, "Life of Madame Guyon, Book 3, Chapter 18, Verse 19."
174. In the original document the footnote reads, "Life, Book 3, Chapter 19, verse 8."
175. In the original document the footnote reads, "18th Book, Quietism."
176. Beaumelle was proven to have forged documents in writing his history of Madame de Maintenon. The distinguished literary scholar, Théophile Lavalée published the story of La Beaumelle's fictitious account of Madame de Maintenon's life in 1865 in the preface to *Correspondance Générale de Mme de Maintenon*. This anonymous author's accusations of La Beaumelle's inaccurate history have proven correct. *Ed.*
177. In the original document the footnote reads, "Memoirs de Maintenon, Book 4, Chapter 7."
178. Father La Combe (1640-1715) was a member of the Barnabite order. He was accused of being under the influence of Molinos and was incarcerated on October 3, 1687. Madame Guyon's first arrest happened on January 29, 1688, shortly after the arrest of Father La Combe. Father La Combe was never released from prison and died on June 29, 1715. *Ed.*
179. Abbé Phelippeaux was a priest with Jansenist tendencies who Bishop Bossuet sent to Rome as his representative. He worked in Rome, along with Bishop Bossuet's nephew Abbé Bossuet, to try to get a condemnation of Archbishop Fénelon and his writings. *Ed.*
180. In the original document the years reads 1705 instead of 1703. This is clearly a mistake because the author has just written that she was cleared by the Issy conference in 1700 and released from her imprisonment three years later.
181. In the original document the footnote reads, "Life, Book 3, Chapter 21."
182. This reference is to Gabriel-Jacques de Salignac, Marquise de la Mothe Fénelon. *Ed.*
183. In the original document the footnote reads, "Volume 4, Letter 11."
184. The author leaves a space in this handwritten document apparently for the name to be added later. No name is in the space. This author is referring to Lord Deskford from Scotland who was a follower of Madame Guyon and lived with her in Blois. The anonymous author refers to Lord Deskford as Lord Chewinkle which is a different spelling of the town Kinlochewe in the area of Scotland where Lord Deskford lived. The anonymous author also appears to change the spelling of Chewinkle during his writing of the document. At times the author writes Chewinkle, Chewikle, and Chewingle. *Ed.*
185. In the original document the footnote reads, "Canticle Volume 4, Section 4, Poem 19."
186. In the original document the footnote reads, "She said while walking in her room to one English man the 5th heroic poem contained in the Volume 4 on meditation and under the eyes of Milord."
187. This might be a reference to the 1693 earthquake that devastated southeastern Sicily.
188. This author refers to Madame Guyon's commentary on the Book of Revelation. The handwritten document mistakenly refers to Apocalypse 188, when the author means Apocalypse 18. This has been corrected in the translation. *Ed.*

189. Madame Guyon died on June 9, 1717. *Ed.*
190. In the original document the footnote reads, "Letters, Volume 5, Page 216. 334. Edition of London."

Select Bibliography

Anonymous, *Supplement to the Life of Madame Guyon, Along with Observations on Her Letter to Monsieur Fénelon concerning Madame de Maintenon*, MS. Add, A.24, fols.7v-9r. Bodleian Library, University of Oxford.
Bossuet, Jacques Benigne. *Quakerism a-la-mode*. London: J. Harris and A. Bell, 1698.
——. *Oeuvres oratoires*, ed. Abbé J. Lebarq, 7 vols. Paris: Desclée De Brouwer, 1926.
Bedoyere, Michael de la. *The Archbishop and the Lady*. New York: Pantheon Books, 1956.
Fénelon, François de Salignac de La Mothe. *Oeuvres*, ed. Jacques Le Brun, 2 vols. Paris: Gallimard, 1983.
Guyon, Jeanne de la Motte. *Autobiography of Madame Guyon*. Vols. 1 and 2. Trans. Thomas Taylor Allen. London: Kegan Paul, Trench, Trubner & Co., 1897.
——. *Poems*, trans. W. Cowper, Esq. Hamilton. London: Gall & Inglis, 1881.
——. *A Short and Easy Method of Prayer*. Philadeplhia: Printed by Francis Bailey at Yorick's Head in Market Street, 1789.
——. *The Song of Songs of Solomon, with Explanations and Reflections having Reference to the Interior Life*. New York: A. W. Dennett, 1879.
——. *Spiritual Letters*. Auburn, Me.: Christian Books Publishing House, 1982.
James, Nancy C. *The Apophatic Mysticism of Madame Guyon*. Michigan: UMI Dissertation Services, 1998.
——. *Standing in the Whirlwind*. Cleveland: The Pilgrim Press, 2005.
James, William. *Varieties of Religious Experience.*, New York: Collier Books. 1961.
La Combe, Father. *A Short Letter of Instruction, Shewing the Surest Way to Christian Perfection*. Trans. J. Gough. Bristol: S. Farley, 1772.
Porete, Marguerite. *The Mirror of Simple Souls*. New York: Paulist Press, 1993.
Ramsay, Chevalier. *Life of Francis de Salignac De la Mothe Fénelon, Archbishop and Duke of Cambray*. Published in *Life of Lady Guion*, Vol. 2, Pg. 325-372. Bristol: S. Farley, 1772.
Saint-Simon, Duc de. *Historical Memoirs of the Duc de Saint-Simon*. Vols. 1 and 2. . Edited and Translated by Lucy Norton. New York: McGraw-Hill Book Company, 1967.

Index

Affair of the Poisons, 30, 107
Annihilation, vii, 2-3, 18-19, 23, 29, 39, 42-48, 50, 59, 64, 67-68, 74-84, 99
Anonymous Author, xii, 58-60, 63-68, 74, 77-78
Augustine, 23, 72

Bastille, xi, 1, 10, 36-38, 44, 59-61, 69, 74-75, 78, 93, 95
Beaumelle, xi-xii, 37, 58-60, 85-87, 89-95
Beauvilliers, Paul, Comte de Saint-Aignan, Duc de, 14, 65, 87, 102
Bethune, House of, 87
Blois, 85-86, 93, 95-100
Bossuet, Jacques Bénigne, xi, 1, 3, 6, 11-18, 25, 34, 37, 51-58, 62, 66-70, 76-78, 83, 92-95, 103
Bourgogne, Louis, duc de (Dauphin), 14, 65, 87

Catoz, Mademoiselle, 96-97
Chevreuse, Charles Honoré d'Albert, Duc de, 14, 65, 87-88, 102
Chewinkle, Lord, 98
Court Cenacle, 15, 65, 69, 73, 79

Edict of Nantes, Revocation of, xi, 6, 34, 72

Fénelon, François, xi, 1, 4-6, 11-18, 23, 25, 33-36, 41, 51, 54, 57-80, 85-102
    Defense of Madame Guyon, 14-18
    Maxims of the Saints, 13, 36, 57-58, 69, 77
Followers of Madame Guyon
    England, 36, 67
    Holland, 36, 64, 67, 99, 103
    Italy, 99
    New World (United States), 61, 71, 79
    Philadelphia, 61, 64, 73, 87, 102, 104
Fouquet, Nicolas (Finance Minister), 87
Francis de Sales, 7, 17-18, 22-23, 51, 72

Guyon, Madame 1, 3, 5, 85-104
    Autobiography, 5-7, 9, 10, 12, 16-18, 25, 37, 39-40, 44, 48, 51-54, 66-67, 75, 81
    Biblical Commentaries, 19-20
    Early years, 6-9
    Feminism, 54-56
    Final Years, 95-104
    Friendship with Fénelon, 11-15
    Implicit Theology, 50-56
    Issy Conferences, 15-16
    Infancy of Jesus, 29, 34

Letter to Fénelon, 101-103
Poems, 20-21
Short and Easy Method of Prayer, 11, 17, 19, 32, 34, 39, 43, 61, 66, 67, 72, 81, 82, 88, 91, 97, 99
Song of Songs, 18, 21, 61, 66-67
Spiritual Torrents, 18, 32, 43, 61
Theology of the Holy Spirit, xii, 23, 25-26, 39, 47, 50, 55
Traveling with Father La Combe, 7-10

Harlay de Champvallon, François de, Archbishop of Paris, 11, 15-16, 67
Henrietta-Anne, Princess, Orléans, Duchesse de, 12, 69
Huguenots, 6

Interior Way, 2, 18-20, 23, 25, 42-47, 52, 59, 62-68, 72-80, 85-90, 94, 96, 98-104,

Jansen, Cornelius, 4, 5
Jansenists, 4-5, 70, 76, 78, 88, 90
Jesuits, 5, 71, 76, 78, 90
John of the Cross, 18

La Combe, Father, 1, 8-10, 15, 29-34, 38, 44, 49, 52, 54, 70, 94-95
La Reynie, Gabriel Nicolas de, 30, 36, 41
Lavallée, Théophile, 60
Louis XIV of France, The Sun King, xi-xii, 5, 8, 12-16, 18, 33, 50, 52, 57-63, 69-80, 83, 89, 93-95, 102
    Revokes Edict of Nantes, 6, 33
    Arrests Madame Guyon, 11, 33, 35
    Frees Madame Guyon, 36
    Death, 70

Maintenon, Françoise d'Aubigné, Marquise de, xi-xii, 1, 11, 13-18, 35, 57-68, 70-71, 78, 80, 83, 85-95, 101-104
    Early years, 13
    Character, 58
    Morganatic marriage to Louis, 13
    Friendship with Madame Guyon, 11
    Expels Madame Guyon from St. Cyr, 35
Maisonfort, Madame de la, 88, 91
Marais, Godet des (Bishop of Chartres), 11, 90, 91, 95
Miramion, Madame de, 86
Molinos, Miguel de, 2-4, 10-11, 17, 34, 37, 53, 67, 73, 90

Noailles, Cardinal Louis-Antoine de (Archbishop of Paris), 15

Phelippeaux, Abbé, 95
Poiret, Pierre, 64, 97, 99
Porete, Marguerite, 3, 77
Port Royal, Convent of, 70
Pure Love, 21, 36, 39-43, 50, 62-63, 66, 74, 76-80, 82-83, 100

Quakers, 73
Quietism, xi, 1-4, 10-18, 34, 37, 71, 73-76, 78-81, 94

Index

Ramsay, André-Michel de, Chevalier, 61, 72, 93, 96, 98
Regency, 57, 86

Saint Cyr School, 11, 35, 54, 58, 71, 77, 88, 90-91, 93, 95, 102
Saint-Simon, Duc de, xi-xii, 13-14, 37, 57-59

Teresa of Avila, 18, 29

Vaux, Countess de (Madame Guyon's daughter), 8, 11, 29, 35, 44, 61, 71, 91, 100-101
Versailles, xi, 13, 30, 36, 58, 69-73, 77-79, 83.
Vincennes, 10, 36, 41, 92-94
Voltaire, xi-xii, 58-60, 71, 96

War of Quadruple Alliance, 71
War of Spanish Succession, xi, 69-70

About the Author

Nancy C. James teaches at Marymount University in Arlington, Virginia, and is a priest associate at St. John's Episcopal Church, Lafayette Square in Washington, D.C. She also serves as a chaplain at the Washington National Cathedral. She received her Master of Divinity from Virginia Theological Seminary. She received her Ph.D. in Religious Studies with a specialty in Philosophical Theology from the University of Virginia. James' completed her dissertation on *The Apophatic Mysticism of Madame Guyon*. Her first book is *Standing in the Whirlwind*.

About the Contributor

John M. Graham is the rector at Grace Episcopal Church, Georgetown, in Washington D.C. He graduated from Kenyon College, summa cum laude and Phi Beta Kappa. He also holds a Master of Arts degree from the University of Chicago and his Master of Divinity with honors from the Virginia Theological Seminary.

www.ingramcontent.com/pod-product-compliance
Lightning Source LLC
Chambersburg PA
CBHW021409290426
44108CB00010B/460